The Contemporary Voice:

How We Teach Voice in the New Millennium

Edited by Bruce Wooding

ISBN 0-9539501-2-3

Published by The International Centre for Voice at Central School of Speech and Drama, London.
© Central School of Speech and Drama 2006
Embassy Theatre, Eton Avenue, London NW3 3HY

Cover photograph by Mike Abrahams
Designed by Nimbus Design
Printed in Great Britain by Axis Europe

Contents

1	Introduction	
2	Delegate List and Programme	
3	Introduction to the Day	
4	Afternoon Introduction – Noah Pikes' Speech, Joe Windley on "What is a Voice Teacher" with Vox. Pop.	
5	Voice in the Conservatoire – Excerpts from the discussion	
6	Voice in Higher Education – Excerpts from the discussion	
7	Voice in the Community – Excerpts from the discussion	
8	The Urban Voice – Excerpts from the discussion	
9	Ring Tone vs. Vocal Tone – Excerpts from the discussion	
10	Is the Dysfunctional Voice Becoming Commercial? – Excerpts from the discussion	
11	Plenary – Summation by Chairs of the Discussions of the Day	

Appendices

Appendix 1: Feedback Sheet

Appendix 2: Feedback Returns – Graphs

Appendix 3: Feedback Returns – Comments

Appendix 4: Chair Biographies

Appendix 5: ICV Information

Appendix 6: Abbreviations Used

Chapter 1

Introduction

by Bruce Wooding, Head of the School of Professional and Community Development at Central School of Speech and Drama, and Member of the Advisory Board for The International Centre for Voice.

The book you are about to read is the third publication developed by the International Centre for Voice. It captures the keynote speeches and some excerpts from the round table discussion groups that took place on the day.

I will briefly explain what the International Centre for Voice is for those of you who do not know about us.

The International Centre for Voice was established in October 2000 in order to serve the professional development of teachers of voice and speech.

The principal aims of the Centre are:
- to create and maintain a professional forum, resource base and network for voice teachers and other interested professionals
- to provide training and professional updating for voice teachers
- to promote research and development in the field of vocal pedagogy.

The Contemporary Voice: How We Teach Voice in the New Millennium arose from an idea that Joe Windley had when he returned from a VASTA conference. He felt it was time for voice teachers to continue to come together and begin to consider 'The Contemporary Voice'. The day was organised into round table discussions focusing on diversity issues and considered the issues we face together as a community of voice teachers.

The event aimed to identify our common and muscular language. The participants set out to articulate and express our function and importance in contemporary education. The event enabled the delegates to take time to share and consider their interconnectedness with methods of voice teaching.

Voice practitioners chaired the round tables and each conversation was recorded. The recordings were transcribed and edited to form this book that captures our vocalisation of the issues facing our profession in a culturally diverse and pluralistic society.

Unfortunately we could not publish all the conversations but these have been kept in the ICV archive in audio form and are accessible to members of the ICV.

For the purposes of the publication we have anonymised the contributions made in the discussions, as several of the delegates wanted their opinions to remain so. I do not think this distracts from the comments made. Indeed the conversations capture a moment in time and raise many pertinent issues. I hope that the following chapters will provide useful reflective materials that will be of use to the new and the more established voice teachers as well as those interested in dipping their toes into the waters of voice.

The opinions expressed in the book do not necessarily represent the views of Central or the ICV. They are individual opinions and often are quite diverse and at times in conflict with each other. However, such debate is useful in helping construct a synergy and shared understanding of 'where we are at' as a community of practitioners and researchers and hopefully will help further the framework for UK voice teaching.

I would like to thank the volunteers from our MA Voice Studies course who helped with the smooth running of the day. May I also offer my thanks to two people who made the event possible. Firstly to Joe Windley who came up with the idea for the parameters of the discussion topics and whose expert advice was invaluable in the planning stage. Secondly I would like to thank Sophie Cable who undertook the event organisation. Her great organisation and eye for detail made the event go smoothly.

I hope you will enjoy reading the book.

Bruce Wooding
Head of the School of Professional and Community Development
Summer 2006

Chapter 2
Delegate List and Programme

Delegate List

Lisa Akesson – Freelance

Jane Atkinson – London Studio Centre

Barbara Barnes

Alex Bingley –Voice/Shakespeare Tutor – Italia Conti Academy

Philip Bliss – Voice Teacher, Brunel University / Freelance Corporate and Public Sectors

Jane Boston – RADA

David Carey – Voice Tutor, RADA

Maureen Carey – Vocal Coach, Living Voice

Rebecca Carey – Freelance Voice Teacher

Sarah Case – Head of Voice, Italia Conti Academy

Mel Churcher – Freelance Voice Teacher / Regent's Park Open Air Theatre

Jules Craig – Voice Teacher / Actor

Charlie Cunningham – Project Leader, Knowledge Transfer, CSSD

Andrew Cuthbert – Short Course Tutor, RADA

Simone Dietrich – Vocal Tutor, ACM

Tess Dignan – Voice Tutor, Rose Bruford

Carol Fairlamb – Voice Coach, Italia Conti Academy / Freelance

Katharine Firth – Module Leader, Bristol Old Vic Theatre School / Private, Corporate and NHS Sectors

Phyllida Furse – Royal Northern College of Music, Tutor in Diction and Phonetics & Director of Sound Move

Alida Gersie

Caroline Goyder – Voice Tutor, School of Professional and Community Development, CSSD

David Gwillim – RP Teacher, ALRA, City LIT

Fonta Hadley

Louisa Harmer – Teacher, Voice Coach, Singing & Piano Theory

Lesley Hendy – Freelance Voice Teacher – specialising in voice for teachers/teaching

Caroline Hetherington – Voice Tutor, LAMDA

Jessica Higgs – Voice Teacher British-American Drama Academy

Janet Howd – Freelance Voice Coach

Dewi Hughes – Freelance Voice Tutor

Sheila Landahl – Actor

Rikke Liljenberg – Voice Teacher E15 / Voiceover artist

Liz McNaughton – Voice Tutor for Speech & Song, Phoenix Again / Freelance Voice
    Specialist

Melanie Mehta – Voice Teacher LAMDA & Private / Speech & Language Therapist
    – Guys Hospital

Danielle Meunier – Voice Lecturer, Swansea Institute

Katerina Moraitis – Voice Teacher, CSSD

Yvonne Morley – Head of Voice, LAMDA

Annie Morrison – Voice Teacher, Guildford School of Acting / Speech Therapist

Paul Nicholl – Research Assistant, Knowledge Transfer, CSSD

Rachael Nicholson – Voice Teacher, Guildford School of Acting / ALRA

Catherine Owen – Head of Voice, School of Drama & Creative Industries Queen
    Margaret University College, Edinburgh

Eluned Owen – Voice Teacher, VCN - working with teachers

Nick Owen – Director, Nick Owen Associates – Corporate, Education and Development

Christine Palmer – Head of Voice, Guildford School of Acting

Suzanne Parke

Margaret Pikes – Roy Hart Theatre

Noah Pikes – Roy Hart Theatre

Simon Reeves – RWCMD

Danielle Roffe – Casting Director

Colin Sadler – MAVS Student, CSSD

Sarah Shepherd – MAVS Student, CSSD

Caroline Sherwood-Roberts – Voice Coach / Voice Presentation Skills, Mountview /
    Voice Matters Association

Christina Shewell – Voice Coach

Sarah Simmons – Voice Coach, Corporate / Private

Vivien Slade – Speech and Language Therapist

Gerard Slamon – Voice Teacher / Performer – Singer, Samuel Beckett Theatre

Ros Steen – Lecturer, RSAMD; Theatre Voice Practioner

Gert Terny

William Trotter – Freelance Voice Coach

Leslie Tuckey – MAVS Student, CSSD

Ingrid Uhlen – MAVS Graduate / Voice Teacher

Annemette Verspeak

John Wild – Head of Voice, ALRA / Actor / Director

Claudette Williams – Voice Tutor, CSSD

Rosalind Williams – Voice Teacher, Cygnet Training Theatre

Joe Windley – Head of Voice, CSSD

Bruce Wooding – Head of the School of Professional and Community Development, CSSD

Caryll A Ziegler – Head of Voice, Webber Douglas

Volunteers from the MA Voice Studies Course at CSSD

Sarah Bishop

Patsy Burn

Sam Feree

Charlotte Graham

Stephen Kemble

Sam Mesango

Sally Mortemore

Daron Oran

Sarah Stephenson

Athina Trevlia

Kara Tsiaperas

The Contemporary Voice
How We Teach Voice in the New Millennium

7th January 2006
Timetable

9.30 – 10.00	Registration and Round Table Sign Up Embassy Theatre Foyer
10.00 – 11.00	Introduction to the Day Keynote Speaker – Ros Steen Embassy Theatre
11.00 – 12.30	Round Table Talks 1 New West Block Rehearsal Rooms 3 – 8 1 – Voice in the Conservatoire 2 – Voice in Higher Education 3 – Voice in the Community 4 – The Urban Voice 5 – Ring Tone vs. Vocal Tone 6 – Is the Dysfunctional Voice Becoming Commercial?
12.30 – 1.30	Lunch (meet in foyer at 12.25)
1.30 – 2.00	Afternoon Introduction – Noah Pikes "What is A Voice Teacher?" – Joe Windley Embassy Theatre
2.00 – 3.30	Round Table Talks 2 West Block Rehearsal Rooms 3 – 8 – Same as am
3.30 – 4.00	Plenary and Closing Embassy Theatre
4.00 – 5.00	Buffet and Networking Atrium – Archive available for viewing in Library Seminar Room

The Contemporary Voice
How We Teach Voice in the New Millennium

7th January 2006
Topics Discussed at the Round Tables

Each round table discussion occurred once in the morning, and once in the afternoon. The discussions were guided by a Round Table Chair, these are listed.

1 – Voice in the Conservatoire – Chair: Carol Fairlamb

Who are we training, how are we doing it and why? Is Conservatoire training inclusive or exclusive? How does the teaching feed the industry? Should the quality of an actor be lesser if they can't speak RP, or a range of regional accents?

2 – Voice in Higher Education – Chair: Joe Windley

Is vocal training in HE the same as in the Conservatoire environment? Should it be? Is HE responsible for developing a set of transferable vocal skills in the student? How do we address and develop vocal training for students and student voice teachers in an ever-changing educational/industrial arena?

3 – Voice in the Community – Chair: John Wild

Who needs voice training? Who gets it? Whose voice are we teaching? How does voice training connect to the wider community in terms of disability, ethnic heritage, business, youth/prison work, class, gender etc? How do we address the teaching strategies needed to deliver appropriate training for students from a multi-diverse community?

4 – The Urban Voice – Chair: Claudette Williams

Is the Urban Voice taking over? What is the Urban Voice? Is it a real sound or a myth? Whose voice is it? Is it evolution or regression? How do we teach the Urban Voice? Can we teach the Urban Voice?

5 – Ring Tone vs. Vocal Tone – Chair: Katerina Moraitis

What is the relationship of voice with digital technology? Is digital mass media modifying our perceptions of reality? What are the implications for syllabus construction, teaching strategies, assessment, and styles?

6 – Is the Dysfunctional Voice Becoming Commercial? – Chair: Christina Shewell

What is vocal dysfunction? How do we define it? Can it be achieved for commercial/artistic purposes? If so what are the implications for training? Should we be aiming to train vocal chameleons?

Chapter 3

Introduction to the Day

Ros Steen, Keynote Speaker

I am very honoured to have been asked to give the opening address to what should prove a very interesting day's discussion about how we teach voice now. Because how we have taught it in the past, even in the last five years is no longer wholly appropriate – the world in which we teach is changing too rapidly for that – nor can we see how we should be teaching in five years time, for the same reason.

From the outset I should say that I have no special crystal ball that enables me to see any further into the future than any of you. Nor can I provide a complete set of answers to the six discussion topics posed. I don't teach in Higher Education directly, for example, nor am I sure exactly what is meant by a commercial dysfunctional voice so I look forward to being informed by my colleagues about these areas.

I can say something about voice and technology, as I train re-speakers who use voice recognition software to subtitle programmes for the BBC. Re-speakers have to listen to programmes and immediately voice everything they hear as it is being said live, for example, a news broadcast including all the interviews or a sports commentary. The process leads them to talk a little bit as a computer does: the voice is devoid of much of its expression, words are clearly cut up from each other and as they speak, *comma*, they have to insert punctuation, *comma*, in order for the subtitles to make grammatical sense when they are read, *full stop*. As yet the re-speakers are able to keep their job speak and their life speech separate; whether there will be long term changes to the voice it is too early to say!

I have done some work within the wider community with different types of groups – community drama groups, those who are differently-abled, people with business or non-acting backgrounds, those from ethnic communities, teachers and drama tutors – although I tend to operate in two main arenas, a conservatoire for drama training, the Royal Scottish Academy of Music and Drama, and the theatre profession. So my talk will largely draw on my experience of teaching voice in these last two contexts but the principles that I believe will guide us in teaching voice in the new millennium apply equally to every context in which we teach.

I am fortunate that my work is in constant demand but I know that this would not be happening if I wasn't offering something of value to people today. In our current theatrical and educational climates money is tight – when was it not? – and nobody, well certainly not the canny Scots, will part with a penny of their precious resources to employ me if what I do does not help them now. The voice work that people want from me has led me to break new ground for myself as a voice teacher, a theatre voice professional and a person, and is beginning to make its contribution to the cultural life of my nation, Scotland.

My path may not be yours but whichever path we take there are four map directions which we must keep consulting if we are to move forwards. However, before I talk about map directions we must know where we want to go. We must start with our vision, whatever that is (and I will say something about mine later on) as this must be our guiding star, the clear end in sight towards which we are journeying. Keeping that in front of us will lead us to take the roads we take, to seek out people who inspire us to go on and to find others to partner us along the way. What is your overall vision in your work, whether for theatre, acting training, teacher training, or the section of the community you are working with? What do you want to see happen in your work context? Because we can make it happen, in time.

The four map directions are:
- Who am I? Because who you are in your work is probably the most significant factor in the whole business of teaching
- Who stands in front of me?
- What is the context in which we are working?
- What is the conversation about?

To explain the last. When I was a young teacher, I thought there were 'things' I had to teach – breathing, resonance, articulation and so on. Teaching was about transferring what I knew to others so they knew it too. Until a fortunate meeting with an education specialist, Bart McKendrick, put me right. He said – and I've never forgotten it – education is not about imparting knowledge. Education is a conversation between two generations, or two parties, about what is important. Hence my fourth question: what is the conversation about?

Who am I? I am Ros Steen and I studied drama at the Royal Scottish Academy of Music and Drama and Glasgow University. After teaching at the University and in Adult Education I became a Lecturer in Voice at the RSAMD 23 years ago, which is where I currently teach. Since 1988 I have also worked as a voice coach, dialect coach, voice director and latterly co-director, pioneering the use of voice work as a medium of rehearsal in professional theatre. I have now taught a generation of actors and have worked on much new writing over many years, being closely associated with the current generation of writers in Scotland including David Harrower, David Greig, Nicola McCartney, and Linda McLean.

As a student I started my journey in voice with the work of Greta Colson, and A.C.Gimson, if that means anything to some of you! So my own training was in the mainstream British tradition. As a young teacher, I undertook some courses with Cicely Berry and they had a strong impact on me for which I will always be grateful. But I felt there was something missing in my work. I didn't know what it was. I just knew there was something else I needed to know.

Then, nearly 16 years ago now, I met Nadine George, formerly of the Roy Hart theatre but at that point working as an independent practitioner. She had drawn on her past experience to develop her own work and technique which she applied to classical text and the training of young actors, a process she recently described in an article for the latest VASTA journal, *Shakespeare Around the Globe*. [1] I started to work with her on my own voice and have continued to do so to this day. This work was my missing piece of the jigsaw. While Cis's work strongly influenced my approach to helping actors connect with the text in practical ways, George's was crucial to a profound understanding of the nature of the voice and its direct channel into the heart of the acting process. The voice research as practice in which I am currently engaged lies at the meeting point of these two traditions.

In recent years, I have been a Guest Lecturer in Voice at the Athanor Akademie in Germany. Being at a distance geographically and metaphorically from what I otherwise take for granted, and working with actors whose first language is not English, enabled me to consider what I was doing more objectively and I have written about this in the current VASTA journal. [2]

But there is another important part of the answer to who I am.

I micht hae waled anither leid for ma speak the day – I might have chosen another language for my talk today – but gin I had anely blethered tae yis aw in Scots – but if I had only spoken to you all in Scots – ye wid shairly no hae liftit my meanin clearly eneuch – clearly enough. Aiblins I dinna spik lik this the hale time – perhaps I don't speak like this the whole time – but I thocht it meet – fit – tae gar ye hear something in yin o Scotland's three heidmaist leids – to let you hear something in one of Scotland's three foremost languages, Scots, (the ither twa bein English and Gaelic). I jalouse – I suspect – it micht gie a wheen o ye – some of you – a wee stound – a wee stab, a wee poke – to ken that Scotland is indeed anither kintra – another country – raither than juist the bit at the tap o England but it is, and kenning that – knowing that – is fair essential tae any unnerstaunding of British theatre the day.

I want to say more about what's happening in Scotland later but it seems pertinent to consider, in passing, issues of national identity and heritage which have a clear connection to voice today. Scotland on Sunday columnist Magnus Linklater said recently,

> In the aftermath of the July 7th bombings and the race riots in France, an urgent debate surrounds the question of national identity [3]

and he asks if multiculturalism has failed. Should being British be addressed more assertively and if so, what does 'being British' stand for? What does a British voice sound like? The Gaelic musician, Donnie Munro, himself a member of a minority culture within Scotland, argues that he is happy to genuinely celebrate other cultures but that we should have more access to our own cultures if we are also to bring something to the table. Shakespeare spoken in RP in Scotland today is practically extinct – our own voices, our own accents have come of age.

I've just recently been in India, and visited the Gandhi museum there. Written on the wall was the following:

> I want the cultures of all lands to be blown about my house as freely as possible. But I refuse to be blown off my feet by any. [4]

Who stands in front of you? Why are they there, what do they want to know, and where are they in themselves? Two main groups of people stand in front of me, students and actors.

Let's start with students, as these are not just our actors of the future, but the teachers and drama trainers too. Young people today are living in a different world, from when some of you, my younger colleagues, were students and certainly from me. A recent survey carried out by the Priory, which specialises in treating mental health problems and addictions, found one in five girls – one in five – between the ages of 15 – 17 had self harmed, alongside "unacceptably high" levels of mental distress associated with bullying and violence in the home. More teenagers were contemplating suicide than ever before and more were being pressurised into sex at a younger age. [5]

The number of women (but not only women) who have a difficult relationship with their bodies and/or their sexuality means voices are, quite literally, disconnected from bodies. The number of men (but not only men) who are afraid to tap into real feeling for fear of being vulnerable, being exploited or 'uncool' means voices cut off from felt life. Schools are now being asked to <u>teach</u> emotional literacy. Eight different advisory documents have been sent to primary schools from the Department for Education and Skills detailing the emotions that are to be taught and how to teach them. It's a different world.

There is so much to deal with before we can get many of our students to any kind of point of balance from which they can begin to work. This takes us beyond lamenting that much of today's speech is inflected upwards à la California high school, meaning we have to teach the resolved cadences at full stops once taken so for granted. It goes beyond auditioning students for entry to drama schools that are so under-energised in their pieces that communication fails, or bemoaning the lack of voice training in teacher training programmes. Our young people – and our students are often the most *fortunate* of our young people – are not confident, at heart, regardless of the tough exteriors. When I compare them to their German counterparts, I wonder just what our education system is up to. Young people today, the leaders of tomorrow, have a profound need to be taken seriously, to be listened to, to be above all validated and helped to find their self-worth. Fortunately helping people to find their voices literally and metaphorically is our territory and we must celebrate the fact that as a voice community we not only do a crucial job, we do it marvellously. My evidence? I rarely meet anyone teaching voice who does not care deeply about it and is passionate about the difference it can make to people's lives. To a person we approach things whole-heartedly and positively. What we have to give is needed, perhaps now more than ever.

Faced with these changes in people, my voice work <u>had</u> to change. Life is difficult in the 21st century and it's not my job to make it more so. Most of what I do now is provide a space for people to, if not let go, put down their stress for a while in order to re-connect with their energy and creativity; with who they are. I haven't taught breathing for a long time, no holding and counting, days of the week – none of that. Just the hardest thing of all. Breathing out. Other exercises come from another time and must be re-thought to ensure their relevance.

With regard to actors, as voice practitioners we just need to be aware that the acting community is stratified, to quite a large extent, by age and training. I'd be interested to know if you've found the same – in my experience I find there are roughly three main groups of actors.

The first, the relatively older actor – perhaps fifties onwards – had the last access to a Rep system where they learnt their craft. Their voices are generally strong and resonant from speaking in large spaces and they tend to absorb a note by trying it out in their voices right away rather than writing it on their script. They have found their own way of doing things and may be reluctant to relinquish that for more contemporary ways of working. At best they have much to share with other members of the company by example and at worst they can do their own thing with very little real transmission between themselves and others.

Then there are the young actors who are heavily influenced by TV and film, stuck quite often in a prevailing though pedestrian naturalism. Anything energised or heightened 'doesn't feel right', is not 'truthful' or 'not me'. Sound familiar? They have yet to learn stamina and professionalism perhaps but are open as a rule and willing to try what they are being asked to do without the sometimes time-consuming discussion which can hold up rehearsal. They often scrawl copious notes on their scripts which can paralyse them when they come to act.

The middle generation actors – mid twenties to late thirties, early forties are a most interesting group – enough experience and professionalism to work seriously but, in the case of the best of them, still open enough to take on board other ways of working. They know what they can do: what they are interested in is what else is there for them. They generally make good ensemble members who can tune into both the other groups and it is these actors who continue to work on their professional development in the voice workshops I run independently.

It is not unusual to have all three groups of actors within one company and while there is much good work, we do sometimes see productions where the disparate acting styles have failed to cohere into a unified world. Obviously we must address each group in a way that speaks to them, but we also have to find a way to channel these different energies and approaches to run together.

The voice work I do, and I'll say something about it in a minute, can be entered at any level of experience and has the advantage of giving these different groups of actors a shared process and a common energy. However, one must be realistic. It is not always possible to work in this way. Some actors are not open, regardless of age (though I find that directors are beginning to take this into account when casting) and equally, one has to respect that more experienced actors might regard such company work as 'school' and are affronted by being asked to do it, in which case one has to cut one's losses. But this is why I believe we have to build a new way of working from the ground up, from training onwards, and have patience for the long game.

Whoever stands in front of me, and whoever stands in front of you, we have to inspire them to do their best, not to please us, but to be all they can be. We cannot make them more talented than they are, but we can help them to fulfil the talent they have and equip them to carry on working without us. And one very difficult thing. We to have find a way to work with people who are more talented than we are ourselves, being careful not to reduce them to our level.

What is the context in which we are working?

I mentioned earlier that we cannot simply borrow from the past and use it to meet the future. We have to appraise what we do in the light of what we want to say through our teaching – to test it against our vision. There is nothing new under the sun but we have to be careful that we are not simply recycling other's ideas in an unexamined way. Nadine was the first to say to me 'take the work and use it in your own way', passing it on for development and not simply repetition. I am not Nadine and I am not operating in her context. I am me and can only teach the work refracted through my understanding and sensibility for my context.

A word about the work. The essence of it is the development of four different qualities of voice, two male and two female, which are in every human voice regardless of gender. These qualities are first explored as sung notes, using the fixed intervals of the piano for guidance, and then as speech in a way that enables actors to embody the text, literally; that is, the whole text is vibrated through the body and voice of the actor and transmitted to the body of the listener. Rather than the text remaining at an intellectual level or felt emotionally and then 'acted', it is connected deeply to where the voice actually comes from: the body source of the creative energies and impulses of the actor. The work has been described by one director as *ultrasound for the point of impulse*. It is an approach that puts the body and voice rather than the head back at the centre of the acting process and rehearsal.

For young actors – actually for all actors really – the voice work not only quickly and simply helps them to confront and accept their own particular body and voice it also directly addresses how they work, that is, what it is that facilitates or limits what they permit themselves to accomplish. The desire to be creative and exciting is often tempered by the fear of exposure that these things imply and the balance of risk to comfort is one that has to be negotiated all the time. This voice work holds young actors, at this often-insecure stage in their lives within a clear, safe structure that allows them to go into themselves, bit by bit, in order to explore and embody that exploration securely.

The first context I had to find a place for the work was in a conservatoire within a fairly traditional Voice Department, which, although it played an important part in the life of the School was still seen by some as a 'skills' department (voice as compartmentalised classroom subject) that 'serviced' the acting courses (voice as handmaiden to the production). I wanted voice work to be integral to the rehearsal process (and I didn't mean just a quick warm-up before the real business) or voice staff would never be seen as the full partners in the creative process I believed they could be. The solution for the department came from my second context, my work in the profession.

Over the last decade or so, I have been fortunate in forging partnerships with open-minded directors who have been willing to give their rehearsal room over to me for the sake of what the voice work can offer them creatively. One such partnership has been at the internationally renowned Traverse Theatre in Edinburgh where I have worked with

Artistic Director Philip Howard to develop theatre practice in which voice work became a medium of rehearsal. For twelve years now Philip and I have been collaborating, learning as we have gone along, and in 1990 we co-directed a production for the Traverse in conjunction with the Barbican Theatre.

How we collaborate is probably a talk in its own right but to give you a thumbnail sketch:

We have an initial conversation about which areas he is seeking help with based on the nature of the text, his thoughts about the writing and the actors he has cast. Then, each day before I begin any voice work, I lead a conversation with the actors about their agenda items and concerns with Philip listening. This means I can take the temperature of the rehearsal room but also I try to reconcile what the actors are after, what Philip is after and my own agenda items – what I think is going on in the text musically, say – so we arrive at the most useful things to work on by consensus. Next we do the voice work – breathing, 4 qualities, individual work for each actor on voice leading into text, directed by me, sometimes physically in the space – while Philip observes and listens. We pay particular attention to the actors' reflections on what the work has done. Philip might then talk about the work's connection to what he is interested in developing, or he might take what has happened and immediately stage it, or he might add a further practical suggestion to be tried then and there. Sometimes the actor's discoveries are all that needs to happen and he simply moves on. All the time we are 'checking in' with one another and reading each other to ensure that together what we are doing remains useful to the actors.

Collaborating with directors in this way let me see a way forward for voice in the conservatoire context. At the RSAMD all acting students undergo a rigorous training in every aspect of voice but in the first year technical work is mainly mainstream. However, towards the end of the year, students begin to study George's vocal technique introduced by George herself. Throughout the second year, I continue to teach the work and at the end of the year it is fully integrated into the rehearsal process of the Shakespeare productions which are the core of study of the summer term. Some of these are co-directed by me and an acting colleague, integrating the work of the two departments in the rehearsal room.

Co-direction is not something undertaken without knowing your partner very well – how they jump, as it were, and it requires a shared vision. Potential contradictions are ultimately resolved one way or another out of trust and mutual respect. You have to learn to separate what you want from what you would go to the wall for. And at that point (the wall) if the depth of feeling is strong enough, one of us will cede to the other. So far we have always worked it out so that we can both buy into the resulting production, a production that we both own as well as the actors. Incidentally, we have found that this way of working does not, in fact, confuse the students! Arguably they learn the most valuable lesson of all, that there is not one truth in acting but many.

My third context is Scotland, where I live and work. It has been my choice not to move elsewhere in order to contribute my life's work to the cultural life of my country. Two years ago, the Scottish Executive, Scotland's devolved Parliament, gave funding for the establishment of a National Theatre, a commissioning body with a remit to provide a showcase for the best of Scottish theatre and to create work of international significance which would represent Scottish culture abroad. A Scottish National Theatre Studio has been set up and I have been approached with a view to bringing the voice work there which would enable me to put my process itself under the microscope. For I am still developing my work, trying to understand it more fully. Can a production be completely rehearsed through the voice work only? I have a conversation to have with myself.

My contexts may not be yours but whatever they are, you have to know how to operate within them while recognising you have the power to create conditions for change. You have the power.

Often what is needed is to find the right people to work with, people who are ready to move forward with you and so we come to the conversation. The conversation between two parties about what is important; the conversations that can move us forward as a profession. Over the many years I have been attending voice conferences and gatherings, up to and including this summer's VASTA conference held in Glasgow, I am aware of one constant: that many voice teachers feel that the work they do is insufficiently understood, recognised and therefore valued as a full contribution to the creative process. We know actors are open to what we have to offer and we can often find affinities with colleagues. In the main we must turn our attention to the conversations we need to have with the authorities, whether our education bosses or directors, to move us forward in the new millennium.

As far as education bosses are concerned, great stress is laid nowadays on 'customer satisfaction', feedback mechanisms and evaluation systems, so the *quality* of our work is often our best advocate there. With regard to directors, in the end the same is true, but there are particular considerations here. We know that relationships between voice people and directors, while being very fruitful in many cases, are not always unproblematic. Difficulties are likely to arise because we share the common territory of the interpretation of the text more closely than any other members of the production team. Certainly the territory of the voice specialist is, as Cicely Berry has articulated, an ability to listen and hear words with a heightened awareness of their underlying sound, rhythm, cadence and form, along with an ability to open this out physically and imaginatively and in this way allow it to inform meaning. [6]

But, if we come clean, this is not all we do and voice work cannot be entirely divorced from interpretation. For that reason there is the potential for a clash of readings of the text and therefore a clash of roles which could prove disastrous. That we as a profession have assiduously avoided such a collision course is a commonplace but I don't think it has been achieved without some risk to our own voice as creative practitioners. In finding new ways of sharing the territory of the text with directors I am not frightened that my work borders on direction. Borders on it, but isn't. By physically opening up the possibilities inherent in the text in rehearsal, my excavation of the text in the voice becomes a creative contribution to the director's excavation of the text, not a challenge to it.

But however we as theatre voice practitioners work – let me nail my colours to the mast now – we have got to get our work out of rooms into where it matters most – the badlands of the rehearsal room. We need to put our work and ourselves on the line if we are to work with directors in new ways. Directors, for their part, must move as well, even if it means calling into question the traditional hierarchies of relationships in theatre. If we want to realign the working relationships in the rehearsal room we are questioning how theatre is made today. And not everybody wants to have that conversation with us. But if it is allowed that there are two stories told when the audience watches a play – the story of the text and the story of the production process – then the change of relationships within the rehearsal room influences the finished product itself. New theatre for a new millennium. And for that reason, perilous though the voyage might be, it is worth undertaking, and we must find partners willing to sail out with us into uncharted waters. There will always be those who will never want to work with us in these ways but this, I suggest, is a temporary blow to our *amour propre*. Let us dust ourselves down and move on. From my experience, more and more directors are coming onside and one must look to converse with the up-and-coming directing generation as a matter of priority.

To finish. My guiding star for a long time has been my vision for theatre in Scotland: the establishment of a generation of trained actors and directors who not only share a common understanding and language of theatre but a shared <u>practice</u>. In this new millennium I have begun to hold workshops for writers and directors who are coming to do the same voice work as the actors in order to understand what it can offer them in their particular roles. I don't know where it will lead but it is happening and I must stay responsible for it and keep on.

And so must you – take responsibility for what is happening and keep on.

Have a vision – know where you are journeying to.

Keep consulting the four map directions.

Take people with you by the excitement and quality of what you do.

All of us, whatever voice journey we are on, must mairch forrard – forward, kenning wha we are, wha staunds afore us and whit the collogue – the conversation – is aboot, wi the licht of the sterns in our hairts, mynds and een – with the light of the stars in our hearts, minds and eyes, looking oot ontae, as yet, unkent airts – unknown horizons.

[1] *Shakespeare Around the Globe* ed Mandy Rees. Pub VASTA, Incorporated Cincinnati 2005 pgs 33-42
[2] ibid pgs 43-58
[3] *Linklater's Scotland.* Article in Scotland on Sunday, Nov 27th 2005.
[4] The Mahatma Gandhi museum, Delhi.
[5] *Sense of failure: the scale of teenage self harm* by Mark Honingsbaum. The Guardian, November 28th 2005
[6] Reference given by Cicely Berry for Ros Steen's application for an AHRB grant for research into the arts.

Chapter 4
Afternoon Introduction

Noah Pikes' Speech

JOHN WILD: The last time I spoke in front of my peers at the VASTA Conference last year, I was absolutely bowled over – this is what I said to them – I'm absolutely bowled over by your enthusiasm, your commitment to voice and your willingness to share ideas openly. I also then went on to say how saddened I was that we had so many talented practitioners in the UK, and we weren't holding our own conference. From that, Joe grabbed me, and obviously Bruce has done some excellent work, and we are all here today. Bruce, Joe and everybody else deserves a huge round of applause. *[Applause]* Of the last two years, I've spent two summers working in Europe with various practitioners to learn new ways, to find new ways of sharing and opening up students' voices, their bodies and themselves. While I was over there, I asked if he would be interested in doing work over here. The irony of this discussion that we had was that all the tutors that I work with in the Roy Hart Centre in Malerargues in the south of France, it originated in London, just down the road in Belsize Park. And I was absolutely flabbergasted why nobody continued to work here or give regular workshops. So I asked him to come today, and he's very kindly paid for his own flight over, to give a chat to introduce you to the ideas and philosophy behind the Roy Hart Theatre. Over to Noah Pikes. Thank you very much. *[Applause]*

NOAH PIKES: Thanks, John. I have a prepared speech because I've been accorded ten minutes and I thought that, rather than ramble on; I'd get it a bit ordered. So you'll be seeing me doing that terribly difficult thing, dodging from the written word to the spoken word as best I can. I will attempt to give you a postcard about what is actually a seventy-year-old history as it's relevant to teaching voice in the millennium. As John indicated, back in the 60s, Roy Hart Theatre had its base in Belsize Park Gardens, and many a time I would walk past the Embassy Theatre and the Central School from Swiss Cottage station and wonder "What went on in here?"

My only experience of voice at that time came from my meeting with Roy Hart's studio and his work, because at that time I was a university drop-out in search of identity and meaning, and I started to find it in his studio. I learnt that the human voice is not only that part of ourselves that we use for speaking and singing, but that it's also a dynamic way to learn about what it is to be a human being – that's the biggest thing I got from working with Roy Hart. At the same time it gave me a way to engage creatively with the existention questions I was struggling with, and it gave me a vocation, you could say. Interesting word, vocation! In its time Roy Hart's work was radical and revolutionary. Why? Because it recognised, and continues to recognise, the phenomenon of the human voice to be firstly one of sound. It hears voice as the world of human sounding and approaches it in a spirit of open enquiry, attempting to hear what is actually there before putting the focus too closely on the more specialised uses we make of that sound. It's in the exploration of an individual's capacity to sound that the creative and connecting nature of the voice may be most fully experienced.

Based on Alfred Wolfson's earlier researches of the 1930s, it took voice out of the larynx and the throat and showed that the whole person – body and psyche – was the key to its further development. Wolfson's was by decades the first holistic voice practice in the Western world. He described his vocal vision as "the voice of the future" and foresaw an individual voice capable of spanning all the ranges of classical singing – all the ranges. By the late 60s, Wolfson's student and research successor Roy Hart had not only developed the vocal range of over six octaves (and that has been certified by laryngologists), he had used it in performance. His collaboration with Peter Maxwell-Davies in 1969 on *Eight Songs for a Mad King* – a work inspired by Hart's voice – resulted in the founding-stone of a new genre, now known as music theatre. In the same year Hart's group of students became known as Roy Hart Theatre and soon stunned audiences in France, Spain and Switzerland. As a director, Hart was a major influence on figures such as Peter Brook and Persofsky. The stories of Wolfson and Hart, their research and achievements, as well as what happened to the university drop-out in search of identity and meaning, are told in my book *Dark Voices: The Genesis of Roy Hart Theatre*, of which a new and revised edition has recently been published.

Then, in 1975, Roy Hart Theatre left Belsize Park. A group of some forty-seven individuals from fifteen different countries and from a variety of professional backgrounds, moved to a half-ruined chateau in the hills of the Cévennes in southern France. They did so because their work and achievements went unacknowledged by the UK's cultural and educational establishment, while in France there was much interest. For example, Jack Lang, who has since become both France's minister for culture and minister for education in the past, was the man who first invited the group to perform publicly – and that was in France – and who subsequently took voice lessons from Roy Hart. After two years we began to receive government support. Shortly after our arrival, though, Hart, his wife and a third member of the group were killed in a car accident. You can imagine that left us in a very extraordinary situation. We'd left Belsize Park for the wilds of the Cévennes hills in a ruined chateau. Most of us were not wealthy people. We survived. It's a miracle, looking back on it, but somehow we did it, and this is how.

The late 70s: a time of survival and adaptation to a new country, a new language, a new way of life. The 80s: a time of opening to new disciplines, numerous visits from artists from different parts of the world, exchanges with these different disciplines, and invitations to give workshops in many parts of the world – not the UK. The Roy Hart Theatre performing skills were enhanced and diversified as it created numerous performances and won several prizes. In the 90s came the need for individuals to affirm their individual visions of the work, with many making a base elsewhere. And teaching had become the main activity of most of those founding members. By then other new members had joined the group also, and some have moved on, such as Nadine George, whom we heard about this morning from Ros. It was a difficult time for the Roy Hart

Centre, which has nevertheless continued to offer courses up to this day. Since August last year it has embarked on a course of change in its administration, and of renewal in the form of teaching it offers (a little bit more on this at the end of my short postcard here).

But what does Roy Hart Theatre work have to offer voice teaching in the new millennium? Well, there is a long experience of vocal research and performance, and the documented responses to that work. Roy Hart Theatre work is a holistic work, making bridges between the uniqueness of the individual voice and the universal phenomenon of the human voice in sound. It concerns itself with all forms of vocal expression. It uses an interdisciplinary approach. It recycles vocal rubbish. In the work of freeing the student's voice to reach its full expressive potential, many disciplines are called upon, from classical singing to non-verbal improvisation, from contemporary dance forms to physical theatre, from archetypal psychology to clown work.

It has developed a unique form of listening to voice – I think that's what Ros particularly underlined, this need for listening. It came up in the group I was in, in "Voice in the Community": voice has two sides. There is no fixed method as such. Each teacher works with the Wolfson/Hart legacy in their own way. Students tell me that, whilst the ways of teaching can be very different, there is something unique and shared in the manner in which all Roy Hart's teachers listen to the students' voices.

Finally, Roy Hart Theatre voice work has demonstrated over more than 40 years that it can do the following things: it can extend the expressive range of the individual voice – that is, through training to develop flexibility and suppleness, enabling great increases in pitch range, in timbre, in texture and in vocal dynamics. [whispers] To stimulate creativity. [shouting] To bring awareness for voices of others. To appeal to people working in many different professions.

For all of these reasons, it can offer a foundation for many kinds of work with the voice. It is this foundation work that seems to me to have been absent from the beginning in higher education in UK voice teaching – a teaching that has been held in an aesthetic ideal and narrow ideas about voice's relationship to the body. The wonder of Wolfson's discovery is to have gone beyond beauty in search of authenticity in the sound of a voice – an authenticity, however, that belongs as much to the imagination as to the self, as much to the moment as to the time; the capacity to sound both [singing] beauty and [growling] beast on the same note. The need for such a broad, holistic and interdisciplinary foundation work in voice training has been increasingly recognised in many European and American higher educational institutions. But its introduction in the UK has hardly begun. Hence John's responses and enthusiasm on discovering it. It was partly in an attempt to help that introduction that I wrote *Dark Voices: The Genesis of Roy Hart Theatre*. David Carey, who was then senior lecturer in voice here, described the book as a major work for voice practitioners, as the work of Alfred Wolfson and Roy Hart (and I'm quoting him here) "has had an increasingly felt influence on voice teaching, theatre and vocal performance over the last 25 years", and he felt that little had actually been known or was written about that work, which was true.

In July 2001 David and I collaborated on an international conference and four workshops hosted by the ICV in London, with the aim of revealing further Wolfson, Hart and Roy Hart [Theatre]'s legacy. So far there has been little follow-up in terms of research and collaboration within higher education in the UK. But John's enthusiasm brought me here in search of it.

At this stage in my life I am focusing my efforts on training for those who can benefit from this work in their profession, whatever that profession might be. In recent years I have trained a number of people in Switzerland in its use, and last November I gave the very first training day to a small private group in the UK. As part of the summer programme of the Roy Hart Centre, I will be offering a pilot training workshop for one week in August on training in Roy Hart work, and this will be done in collaboration with Margaret Pikes, who is my sister, who is living in London. Contact her in the networking time if you'd like to have an experience of Roy Hart Theatre voice work – she is a founding member also of that group.

In conclusion, let me give you a picture of the centre in France as it is now, 30-odd years on. The ensemble of old stone buildings now has centrally heated performance spaces and several studios, accommodation for visitors, as well as homes for several of the members. All of this is set in a magical unspoiled landscape with its hills. It would be great to see you there. And at the same time in the centre there are moves going on to change the administration, to get the place set up with an internationally accredited programme of work. It has largely gone on in an unaccredited way, although we attract post-graduate students from America quite a lot, from European countries. Many of us have been teaching in university-level institutions around Europe and America for perhaps 20-25 years, and it's time that somehow we gathered this body of work called Roy Hart Theatre together, got it accredited and protected its intellectual property, because it's been a great influence but in some way it hasn't fed back into the Centre, and it's time we preserved some of that original research for posterity – and for you. Thank you. *[Applause]*

Joe Windley's Presentation of "What is A Voice Teacher?" – Video

One should hesitate before speaking a sonnet on a snatched lunch, on only a few hours sleep. I will be quick. We have something to show you before we break out into our groups once again. Forgive me, Shakespeare.

Sonnet 64

When I have seen by Time's fell hand defaced
The rich proud cost of outworn buried age;
When sometime lofty towers I see down-razed
And brass eternal slave to mortal rage;
When I have seen the hungry ocean gain
Advantage on the kingdom of the shore,
And the firm soil win of the watery main,
Increasing store with loss and loss with store;
When I have seen such interchange of state,
Or state itself confounded to decay;
Ruin hath taught me thus to ruminate,
That Time will come and take my love away.

This thought is as a death, which cannot choose
But weep to have that which it fears to lose.

A love that we perhaps all share, that of voice and people. Let that sit for a moment.

I wanted to start with that because it captures something essential about the changing nature of the world, our world, and demonstrates the ancient nature of the matter of change. How we consider our world, in terms of natural sciences, cultural and sociological patterns, faith, family or politics, we're all subject to the evolutionary forces of erosion and deposition – the battle between the land and the sea. The shoreline is a restless boundary. By definition, it is a cutting-edge location. At that place we can perceive how the elements perpetually engage in discussion upon the subject of change. A cliff-base, for us, can be a useful metaphor to support established concepts in voice teaching. Follow this notion through and we can conceive how the rock strata in sequential layers could be made up of posture, breath, onset, tone, pitch range, resonance, articulation, language, text, expression, acting, presentation. Some layers of that rock are more durable than others and help to keep shape and form to the cliff: breath, posture, expression, resonance. Others seem less resistant to the forces of change: accent, clarity, acting. These layers are more easily influenced by the sea of change which consists of fashion, politics, music, technology, entertainment, advertising, affluence. The current values of art and entertainment seem very much conditioned by a lack of definition and the prevalence of fluidity, the minimalism of contemporary performance, the sense that anybody can be a celebrity, and the appearance of "performance democracy" through accessible digital technology.

The current marketplace for actors is obsessed with reality and minuscule representation. It's not necessarily invalid, but it's certainly there as an obsession. To survive, actors need to be able to morph into roles which do not bear the hallmarks of training. In effect, the actor must be subtle and fluid, must migrate to a place of shifting sandbanks, rather than be located at the solid rock outcrop.

Where does that leave the voice teacher? Learning to swim, I think. *[Laughter]* We as voice practitioners are at the cliff-face. We look out to sea, and with fear are mindful of the projected outcomes of global warming. We observe the way in which the cliff is eroding. The certainty of rock outwitted by the fluidity, volume and movement of the sea, from mighty natural monolith to grain of sand. Yet the grains of sand still contain the elements found within the cliff. The fundamentals of voice remain. After erosion, under turbulent waters, the grains of vocal sand, still with their constituent parts, accumulate and reform, eventually becoming rock once more. That new rock characteristically reflects the forces exerted upon it and the processes that shape it. To understand the relationship between sea and shore in terms of voice is: to know as much as possible about the empirical aspects of our subject, and to be fully conversant with the changing nature of society. If this balance can be achieved, if we can perceive and utilise the powerful forces of erosion and deposition, if we can clearly see how our work and knowledge is part of society, we can create a second in which our pedagogy can serve the ancient truths of human communication and function at the cutting edge of sociological and cultural evolution.

Bearing this in mind, on the Voice Studies course, along with developing the necessary practical and eternal skills, we've been investigating the role and function of the voice teacher in contemporary society. In order to do this we need to get our feet wet. So we've been speaking to the public – it seemed like a good idea. What you're going to see now is a brief video with responses to a few key questions that will be illustrated on the screen, so I won't set them up for you now. We had over five hours' worth of recordings. There is an awful lot of material that we could have brought to this, but we didn't. This is our video as is. It's out there, it's on the street, it's not massively tidy, but make of it what you will.

Video

Have you heard of a Voice Coach - what do you think a Voice Coach does?

- I have no idea what a voice coach does.

- I think it's someone who could help you with singing, public speaking, acting... something like that?

- I have heard of voice coaching, but I don't really know – I don't know exactly what they do.

- I have heard of a voice coach, and I think I know what a voice coach does, but I'm not 100% sure.

- Erm, no, not exactly.

- They can help someone with the pronunciation [sic] and I think they also help with the elocution, of how you pronounce words and how you come across to people, but I'm not 100% sure. I always think I do, but then it gets put towards me, I'm a bit, kind of like, shy away from it.

- I think a voice teacher is probably someone who helps people who have speech impediments or maybe a lisp or something like that, or maybe someone who is going to go into singing and needed some sort of coaching. Around about those sort of lines.

- Seeing as I've never heard the expression "voice teacher" in my life before, I would have no idea what a voice teacher does.

- I think they... I know they're involved in drama.

- Someone who, I suppose... oh! It's difficult to sort of identify what a voice coach is.

What do you think a Voice Coach would teach?

- I would guess that a voice coach helps you with your speech and singing.

- I think it's about teaching people how to use their voices effectively when communicating to the public, be it live public or on radio or on camera, I imagine.

- I think a voice coach helps people with a range of problems. It could be anything from speech therapy to somebody with... God, is it...? I sound terrible! Things like lisps and things like that, to kind of help them through their problems. I do think they can help someone express themself a lot better than they do already. And…what do I think they should do? I don't know. I honestly don't know. I'm not in that field, I just haven't got a clue about it.

🖋 I think a voice coach is maybe trying to get the information from different sources, and then maybe to analyse what every individual has got about their voice coach. But in effect I don't know what the voice coach actually does.

🖋 I suppose to get people to speak, to help people to speak properly, in inverted commas. So in English language, that'll be to… pronounciation [sic], maybe help them with vocabulary, things like that. That's as far as I could guess.

🖋 I think a voice teacher guides people and teaches them how to make the most of what they've got in their voice.

What would you ask a Voice Coach to help you with?

🖋 I'd love for a voice coach to teach me how to sing properly.

🖋 If I could work with a voice coach, I think I'd improve my public speaking technique for… so I could do better presentations and stuff.

🖋 I've got no idea. I don't know, I really don't know.

🖋 I think to be taught how to, sort of, think before I speak would be a very useful tool for me, for sure. I don't know if that's something they could help with, but…

🖋 Maybe to make their voice sound very nice to people to listen to. Because some of the voices are very coarse and somebody would like to hear a very nice voice from their partner, and that sort of stuff. Yeah.

🖋 Erm… I wouldn't know what… I'd ask them to listen to my voice, or maybe a recording of my voice, and ask them how my voice could be improved and how that would help me in my life, for my voice to be improved.

Do you think a Voice Coach could help with cross-cultural relations?

🖋 I think working with a voice coach would help cross-cultural relations and communication, because it would give you a better insight of how to make yourself more easily understood.

🖋 I don't know if voice coaching could help that. I think that's helped by understanding more about other people's cultures and how they communicate and how they… I don't know how voice coaching comes into that. I'm not sure.

🖋 I think that communication is the key to cross-cultural relations, so yes; I think it would definitely help.

🖎 Certainly, because the purpose for this is to really they can understand what you're talking about.

🖎 In terms of arguing, if people would be able to communicate better, I think that they'd understand each other a lot better, and that this will be less conflicts, and erm… it's just really, sometimes it's kind of upsetting when you're trying to explain something to someone and they're feeling offended when you… because they can't understand what you're saying because they haven't heard of a word that you've used or something silly like that.

🖎 By getting them to put their beliefs aside, and knowing that everybody has a voice and can use it for friendship and sharing common goals.

🖎 I always think that a voice teacher would probably, probably should be more encouraged to go out a lot more, meet people from different cultures, different societies, the way they speak. My friend, she's from Nepal, and she talks very proper, proper English, and she's very calm and collected from the way she speaks, plus she also believes in Buddhism as well. And since she's done that, the way she views everything is completely different, and the way she talks about it, she sounds a lot confident in the way she talks. Sometimes a bit kiddish as well, the way she talks as well, but that's her personality that she projects with her voice as well. So you can pick up also a lot from everyone around you, how personalities affect how you speak, where you was brought up, the people that they socialise with as well.

🖎 Hmm, interesting. I'm not sure about that at all, to be honest. I'm not sure how important speaking is in terms of getting along. The reason I say that is because a few years ago I spent a month in Japan without knowing a word of Japanese, and somehow I managed to get myself understood and understood what everyone else was doing or saying, etc. So I'm not 100% how important what you're saying is. I think, as far as people are concerned, it's usually more to do with how you look and how you behave and how you move, as opposed to what you're saying and the way you're saying it.

🖎 I think that in 2006 every year the dictionary has changed, and more words are put into it that… New words that are being brought, used with different words, and everyone's perspective of what proper English is has completely changed. From the Victorian days, everyone used to speak a similar way and everyone had a sort of class. These days everyone's very mixed. You have everyone from different classes integrating with everyone else. And people have learnt to learn and adapt with everyone else, and that's the way to move forward. The word "proper" is a word that probably is not used so much now these days. Everyone considers everyone who can speak English correctly and make no mistakes, that would prove more classed as proper, rather than someone who sounds a bit more… like they're a member of the royal family. Yeah.

JOE WINDLEY: OK. That's the problem, isn't it? Each one of those people has dignity, a life, human value – has a voice. Yet we can see that their range of understanding of themselves and their subject is incredibly diverse. We as a species, it would seem, are not terribly well known about. We have some work to do in order to redress that balance and allow these people to maximise their time on the planet, perhaps, if that's not too patronising. I don't think it is.

Chapter 5

Voice in the Conservatoire
Excerpts from the Discussion

Chaired by Carol Fairlamb. Discussion Brief: Who are we training, how are we doing it and why? Is Conservatoire training inclusive or exclusive? How does the teaching feed the industry? Should the quality of an actor be lesser if they can't speak RP, or a range of regional accents?

The excerpts are quoted but not named – people are given letters A-Z. A is Carol Fairlamb, the Chair. Z is a person unidentifiable from the recording.

A: First of all, to clarify what we mean by "conservatoire". I looked it up in the dictionary and it said that originally, of course, it was a musical conservatoire – that's what it refers to back in the 18th and 19th centuries. We started to use this in the acting world at the beginning of the last century, and it came out of the idea of striving for excellence – that's the basic philosophy. Of course now there are many drama schools which consider themselves to be conservatoires, and perhaps not everybody in the world would consider them to be conservatoires, so there is a mixture of things going on there. Just recently, within the last few years, there is the Conservatoire for Dance and Drama which has been formed, and the three drama schools that are part of that are the Bristol Old Vic, RADA [Royal Academy of Dramatic Art] and LAMDA [London Academy of Music and Dramatic Art]. But I suppose what we're talking about is this idea of striving for excellence, but you may have your own ideas about that – it's just a definition before we go any further…

Pedagogy is very much in my mind at the moment. I'm here because I was asked to be here, but one of the things that has been preying on mind since I was asked was something that Sally Grace said to me ten years ago. Sally Grace taught me verse here on the voice course, and she said, when Central were bringing more students in on the acting course, she said: "You know, there are really very few people who can actually do this." That's why we are taking on more and more people. So that's what's in my head, as a question, not as a statement. Maybe that's a way of framing things: as questions rather than answers.

B: What I'm worried about is: why and how can we be training more and more people every year for less and less jobs that there are actually out there for classical actors… even any kind of acting, really, unless it is highly commercialised.

D: …at the moment I'm teaching students who maybe get 24 hours a week instruction, and I find that I'm continually, unintentionally, chastising them that they're not up to speed, that they haven't got the stamina, that they're not committed... And actually it's not fair, because they're not being given that training that would give them those tools. So it's about me being able to... I just feel like I need to be realistic for them, and I don't know what that is, because to me an actor's training is all-encompassing, and is that athletic, and I don't know how to downsize what those core beliefs have been in order to do a good job in the sphere at the moment. I feel that I'm not in the business now of training actors but in the business of making money out of people who want to be actors, and that I find distasteful.

E: "Conservatoire" to me has always had connotations that you are studying the art form, as opposed to going and studying something academically, or training to teach the art form. It is about training in the art form itself.

G: I share the misgivings about whether potential actors are recruited simply as cash cows to keep institutions going. Also, in my working life, the change has been where actors were at least valued when they were employed. Now, it seems to me, among many of the younger producers and directors, they don't actually want actors. They want people to respond to commands efficiently so that they will get their piece of filming or they get their project done efficiently. They want this thing that they call "real". Certainly a lot of my work has been in voiceover work, and where it started out as being 90% RP, middle-of-the-road, I have to say "white male", that's now the minority. It's actually despised. A lot of the younger directors and producers that I work for think RP is posh, think that people like me are out of touch and represent some Anglo elitist little group. And what they want is "real", and what they want often is – it's being discussed in another group – what we might call a dysfunctional voice, a voice that sounds untutored, unproduced, that has some kind of background to it, that might have come out of a club at three o'clock in the morning. Those are the kinds of voices that seem to me to be required now in the name of reality. I'm interested in what a conservatoire is actually doing. Who are they training for? What is this training? What does it consist of, and why?

H: I have also felt the dumbing-down of excellence in the last 25 years. Somehow it hasn't been held up: almost the opposite in schools. Those excellent students are bullied to stop being excellent, so they hid it.

J: I've done a lot of voice work with singers, who, believe it or not, have walloping great voices which they lob forth, but they can't actually use the speaking voice as an instrument. It's a completely different art.

K: I just fear I'm in a crisis at the moment – it seems to me fraudulent work. I work with post-graduates: my numbers have gone up to 43 from 30 last year. And the quality – you mentioned standards of excellence – I mean, it's a travesty. Quite frankly, some of them shouldn't be there. And in fact some of the students have actually said to me in the past, "Why are some of these students here?" ...so much work today is in film and television, and the drama schools aren't doing enough of that. Obviously they're covering it, but maybe it's only a month. Well, there are endless channels. And nearly all the actors say, "I want to work in film and television". So I just feel a real disparity of integrity going on in this training world.

M: Rose Bruford's community theatre arts course is quite different from what we're talking about in terms of conservatoire, so as a teacher I'm interested in that – the different types of training. I don't think I quite understand what the conservatoire is. Another thing to think about is what was brought up as well, about the dumbing-down process, and the question of… if so many people are training nowadays for very few jobs (and I'm talking about actors here), do we have to teach them in order to give them the optimum chance to get the job, or do we let them be creative and explore their creativity. And are those different things or are they the same thing?

N: I started out as a teacher and then trained at Cygnet Training Theatre in Exeter, which is a unique and anomalous member of the Conference of Drama Schools, because we're a functioning company that trains at the same time. We don't take any more than six students a year – Over the years we've looked at all sorts of ways to get funding and that sort of thing, and realised that a lot of courses have become degree courses for funding purposes more than anything else. What frightens me about it at the moment is the number of degree courses that are proliferating without really proper training. People leave them saying that they're actors and they haven't actually had the kind of rigorous training that an actor probably needs.

A: There seems to be a theme, and perhaps I've jolted that into action, that actually what we're doing is dumbing down a little bit, and we are teaching people who we don't believe are going to get work ultimately, and this is a terrible moral dilemma in our lives, not just in our work – that seeps into our whole lives.

E: I thought your point was very good about "are we training people, or are we training them for the workplace, effectively?" Of course that's one of the problems with getting the funding, isn't it? Because once you've got the funding, it almost defines that you've got to train people as a product to sell at the end, whereas my definition of "conservatoire" – I think back to the term last century, when … you went to conservatoire to study what it is you wanted to study without thinking "Then I will get a job and such-and-such".

E: Obviously everyone needs a job at the end, but it can take away a fuller investigation of the craft and skills, because you're thinking about "What can I do that's going to get me that job at the end?"

M: Just this morning we were talking quite a lot about the fact that a lot of people who work maybe aren't even trained. They like to pick people off the streets to do films because that's more "natural", that's more "real". So if people are then going to train and work, what are we training them for? I love the idea of a conservatoire, where people just go to develop their ideas. But then we are a commercial world and people do need to work.

C: I know someone mentioned earlier that the producers and directors these days seem to like to "keep it real", but I think we're in the business, being voice practitioners – remember this is for the longevity of an actor's life, and it may be that this is a short-term thing – but we are in the business of being not just for TV and film, but for the theatre, for open spaces, for bread-and-butter work outside of the "keep it real" soap operas.

C: …there is always the need to push forward some sense of standards, some sense of excellence, and I think that will arise out of the dumbing-down. You will see it in education over the next 15 years. Something has to give, and again we constantly revisit old traditional values.

G: If somebody said to me "excellence", it would be someone who had an ability far beyond average in their craft, whatever chosen craft that would be. Nowadays there is no training ground for actors. The repertory system is dead. I was lucky enough to see it in its death throes – hardly "lucky" – but I was there at the end of it. Without having had that, I would never have had the experience or the freedom to experiment and play with words, with language, tastes and parts that were really delicious in the mouth. I would never have had that chance. On television or film it's *[snaps fingers]* one take and that's it. In the rep, it was every night for three weeks, sometimes longer. Younger actors just do not have that chance to hone their craft. And it is a craft. A craft is something that you can evaluate, it is something that you can put a qualification on it, if you like. But I would say the dumbing-down at the moment is far too academic. This is not an academic craft; it is an instinctive one. There are certain things that can be learnt, there are certain ideas that can be "academicised", if that's a word, but it is a practical thing. It is a doing thing. It is acting. To put a degree on it seems ludicrous to me – I will never understand that. If a conservatoire means keeping degrees out of acting training, then I'm all for them.

M: ...I've just worked with an actor who's worked a lot and she said: "I've considered going back to Central or to Mountview or somewhere like that to do the MA, because then I'll be seen by the right casting directors. Actually, to be honest, it's going back to this training for commercial... Where will I get the work? Where will I be seen by someone? Well, if I've got Central or RADA or one of the... perhaps considered to be conservatoires on my CV, then I'm more likely to be seen more commercially. That's very cynical, but...

E: I think it's perfectly possible to get your skills and craft without going through training, because there are a lot of people out there who've done that, but we know that training gives you space to find out and develop. One of the recurring things that I get at the Actors Centre and in my own private work is that a lot of young people who have come up through TV have only done camera work. In their late teens they're very popular with producers and casters because they're a commodity and they get paid a lot of money. Then they get to their early 20s and suddenly nobody wants them. It makes them feel that suddenly they can't act, whereas before they could. But the bright ones realise that actually they thought they were acting, but perhaps they weren't. And then they search out someone like myself or your own selves to fill in that gap. Then a lot of people say: should I go and do the training so that I've got that space to develop?

I: ...the casting in the third year is such that everybody gets something to do. A senior casting director continues to come through the whole of your final year to watch the shows. You will be seen. But it seems to me – and maybe this is an old person's view – it seems a long way to go just for that, for a lot of them, when in fact quite a lot of them have already done some form of training. It seems a big commitment, both in time and money, to do those courses.

K: ...the class sizes now are so huge. When I was at Guildhall 30 years ago, it did feel like a conservatoire. It was small, it was intense, brilliant! I really felt I learnt my craft. I didn't leave at all feeling "I've got to go somewhere else". I thought: I've had three years of training and I feel now I've got to develop. Whereas today, every voice coach I talk to... You've got too many students to get through the detail of work. ...43 of my students are not going to leave after a one-year postgraduate MA course and go into work – the bottom line. I just want to give them skills with their voice. If they go for any interview, they know how to present themselves. They know how to hold themselves, they know about their breathing, to relax themselves, whatever they're doing, whatever work.

F: I think there is actually something to be learnt from the academic world and the university world in that if somebody goes to do – and as we are now providing MAs and BAs – if somebody goes to university to study a BA, and they go into theatre or any other subject, never does that university say: "And you will work in this field once you get this BA". Never does a university say: "And if you do this MA you will work in this field". What they're saying is: "We will give you the opportunity to explore and discover and learn and find out about that. And some of you, if you're really good or really interested may work in this field, but many of you will go off and work in another field." I don't think there is anything wrong with us saying: "Come learn about theatre, learn what the craft is about, discover that, discover how you relate to that, where you fit in this world – and those of you who are really good will be able to carry on and work in this field. A lot of you won't, but still come explore and enjoy that." I don't see that there is anything wrong with that.

K: But the point is that they're paying £13,000 a year at Mountview for this one-year course. They all want to be actors. They all come with a dream to be an actor.

F: Which is fine, but in the way that the courses are marketed, it needs to be said: "We don't offer you a guarantee", and I think that there needs to be some bravery on the part of the people offering the courses, saying "We will take you, we will provide you with the course. Come and take what you can from that. But we're not saying that you will work at the end of this." I think there does need to be some honesty. If people are taking so many people in terms of saying: "This is what we can offer you. The rest of it, you take and you do yourself."

G: ...when I remember the selection procedure from my first training, it was a hard and gruelling process, among many drama schools. And most people didn't make it. It seems that you're saying now that students are being taken for other reasons than talent, or something spotted by a particular drama school, and that's where the discomfort lies.

L: There are two sides. On the one hand there is a big demand for these kind of courses, because people do want to be able to voice, to stand up and speak text. They do want to have that experience. I suppose in reality a lot of people change. They go on and do other things. They may be related – I'm sure a lot of people do end up in related jobs. That's one side, probably a positive side of it, but the other side is that maybe there should be some kind of distinction – there should be made some distinction – between what is this conservatoire training and is this university drama degree the same thing, or not? If not, then they should somehow be defined. And that students should know what they're going to do.

N: ...our bodies and our muscles learn slowly. Our minds can understand things quickly. For an academic course, you only have to write things down, read them and understand them with your mind. But your body will take three years to be an actor. I feel that it's a distinction that has to be understood and made. It's dishonest to say that you can make an actor of somebody in one year, unless they've phenomenal talent. Without expecting it, they will then have to go on and work at it for longer themselves. At the same time the universities are opening up courses all the time, saying that they're training actors.

C: ...the dumbing-down is so huge, that there is a dumbing-down in the standard of teaching. I'm privy to tick boxes as the students are. And nobody cares whether I do my job brilliantly. They just care that I've taught nasal resonance in week two of term three. There is absolutely a dumbing-down in delivery, because if there is nobody asking you to excel and they are opening out how many students that you are being asked to spread yourself thinly across, then there becomes a kind of self-preservation about how creatively high you're going to fly. The dominance of RP has lost its place in drama schools, and quite rightly, but it means now that it's taught often in non-conservatoire training with as little definition as regional accent in the country. So we recently put on a third-year production of *Restoration*, and it was decided that actually we're not able to do that any more because nobody can do RP – so we'll just cut that out of the whole canon of training. There is doing Restoration in other accents, so that would be an option maybe.

C: ...I don't want to spend my energy locking horns on a personal level with institutions. I want the voice institute to have its own clout and body and set of standards and practice, so that I can just say: "You can't do it, it's not allowed. In the voice world it's not allowed". And not to say: "Because I disagree with it". I don't want it to be a personal agenda, or us all to be fighting individual battles.

A: ...I think that is what this day is about, really, it's about becoming that vehicle for change, that we can do that collectively. Almost everybody in the last group used the word "fighting" at some point, "locking horns", "struggle". And yes, we're all on our own, really. An old principal of mine, who will remain nameless, described us as the "voice Mafia". Which was very funny on one level, but on another level, it just indicated how he felt that he was having to fight his corner against us.

D: As a teacher, I just want to teach. I think of what I do as "in the trenches"? It's absolutely frontline stuff. I will accept that I have to write screeds of pieces of paper if it enables me to teach. But when bodies are saying: "And actually can you do masses of research, because research brings us in money, and therefore we can make the course better..." Well, that's another thing I'm going to have to juggle. ...it's *the* buzz-word in all schools, that they'll get more funding if their teachers are research-active. And the research money does come to you, and it comes to the project you're doing, but the university gets academic credit based on how research-active its lecturers are.

A: Is there anything in the conservatoire, at the beginning of this century, that is positive?

G: It keeps alive part of our culture, and I think that's its greatest advantage. The need for actors to be classically trained has reduced to almost nothing. There is a high-definition role for them in a very small way with some companies. But what we were talking about earlier: the route that most actors took, certainly in my generation, was out into a thriving repertory system in the regions, where they really developed and learned their craft. Three years wasn't enough. Now that isn't the case, but conservatoires can at least be the last bastion the total dumbing-down to produce only people who can – my agent now looks at potential clients with a five-year window. You were talking about a whole career. That's what they're looking at as a whole career now, because people are not expected to have a long shelf-life, they're not expected to mature and grow and move on in roles and move on in productions. But I still defend the conservatoire, to produce people for that small part of our culture that is still thriving. Maybe times will change again.

N: ...I think it's really important to stick by the standards that we believe in, even if the commercial world doesn't recognise it at the moment. Cygnet has been through thick and thin over the years, and it's through the dedication of the two founders, and the willingness to go without money for a lot of the time, that it survived.

A: We look back on the last hundred years with great – I suspect I'm talking for everybody, and forgive me if I'm not – with admiration and respect for what has gone before. In the next hundred years, when another group of people are sitting maybe in this building, talking about what went on in the last hundred years, what would you want them to be saying? What will you hope will happen in the next hundred years?

I: I hope people will say – in the same way that Noah was talking about Roy Hart's untimely death, but it carried on. So maybe we think now is a bit of a dearth period for whatever reason, but actually the people who were around at the time carried on, for whatever reason. ...I think times will change.

K: My hope is that in a hundred years people will say, it's normal practice that voice is taught in primary school. Voice, reading, how to control your voice... wouldn't that be wonderful?

M: I think it's like a torch. Sometimes it burns brighter. And maybe it will burn brightly again.

A: A wonderful thought to end on. Thank you very much, all of you.

Chapter 6

Voice in Higher Education

Excerpts from the Discussion

Chair: Joe Windley. Discussion Brief: Is vocal training in HE the same as in the Conservatoire environment? Should it be? Is HE responsible for developing a set of transferable vocal skills in the student? How do we address and develop vocal training for students and student voice teachers in an ever-changing educational/industrial arena?

The excerpts are quoted but not named – people are given letters A-Z. A is Joe Windley, the Chair. Z is a person unidentifiable from the recording.

A: For the purposes of this: FE/HE. I think we can group them together. From what's happened so far, and the reason why you chose to come to this session, where are you now? What should we be doing with this time that we have?

B: The thing that occurs to me most is that in education there is very little work on voice unless it's instigated by an outside member, not a member of the university. I was married to a man who was a professor at the University of Exeter, and then later at the University of Middlesex, and worked in research. One of the things I was very aware of was that so many people had to go into the lecture theatre absolutely untutored in any way at all. The students sat there and could often not hear anything that was being said, and it was a very unsatisfactory experience from both points of view. I've always felt that if I could help in that area to make it a more satisfactory thing, particularly for the audience – you must remember the audience all the time – then I would like to try to do that. So in my corporate work I do try to do as much of that as I possibly can.

I: Taking that point, I work sometimes with seminars for the lecturers at the universities where I teach. The American university system is very open to this business of public speaking and voice work for the lecturer. But one of the lecturers said to me at one stage: "I've got to be wary of this." When he was going for an interview at university, he said – he's a Canadian – "I've got to be careful not to express myself too well or to communicate too well, because they will doubt my intellectual potential." Having been to some university seminars – I went to one on "Beckett in Performance" at Leeds University for two days, a performance-based seminar – it was incredible, the standard of delivery. It was almost as if somebody had said to those people: "You must not communicate, you must know this is as boring as possible, you must read every word, you must never look at your audience." That was the accepted norm, and as the young Canadian lecturer said to me, he had already assumed that this was the requirement.

A: So how would these things impact upon the role of the voice teacher? What are the challenges that we face if we're to do something about that? Is the challenge just keeping things as they are? Is that adequate? Might be… the status quo that is at work within HE now, is it worth keeping it as it is? Does it function? You know, if it ain't broke, don't fix it – are we saying that something's broken in it? If we are, how can we identify what that is? How could we work together in order to change the situation?

E: I think that's exactly it. We need to swim. It's about swimming in the culture as it is now, not trying to change it, not trying to change the world, but absolutely always changing ourselves. Because we're working on our own voices when we work, and if we're not, then we're very much in danger of just setting up these little islands of expertise, and then becoming fear-ridden ourselves. We have to be in this culture, swimming in it and using it. The more people that are working in corporate work – there are bridges being made all the time: bridges into healing… . We are a very broken society, and the work that we're doing in making ourselves whole – and that's what we're doing, the minute we start to get into our bodies, to try to connect with our own voices, we're making ourselves whole – that's where we have to start. But in doing that, bringing ourselves into whatever area of the work we're in, whether it's university lectures or corporate work or drama schools – we are bringing that healing in with the work itself. But we're only doing it because we're swimming in it. It's a mistake to think, well, I've got to… maybe we do need to write articles, maybe we do need to get into the media more… but that's not the way it works. I think we get into the media by becoming more relevant, by swimming in what's happening at the moment, which is quite dysfunctional as a society.

A: What about the perspective of the student?

L: I think you've got to start with the teacher. Without good models all the way through – we're not just talking about HE; HE is the end, but they start at about two or three years old – if you haven't got good models all the way through, what are you going to have at the other end, coming into HE? So I think we've got to start with the teaching profession as a whole. Training the lecturers – I know who you're talking about, and I've worked with quite a few. But, interestingly, once they knew what I was doing they came and asked me for help. A chap who actually was doing behaviour management, would you believe, actually asking for help on his voice, because he didn't actually have voice as part of behaviour management, which seemed to be completely barking, but there you go. So I think we've got to start with the teachers, we've got to start in HE, in the ITT, whoever is doing teacher training – we've got to get in there. And not just have the two-hour lecture, which they have at the moment. You know, they will say: "Oh, we do voice", and when you talk to an NQT and you say, did you do voice? "Yes." And you ask them what they did… a two-hour lecture.

L: What I would like to see is that, a part of every teacher training package. And they have to now have some sort of… because they're now graded on teaching by their students in universities, so lecturers are coming into this as well. But part of the training – it's not just about how good you are at your subject, it's about how you communicate your subject, and that has to be more than just that one-off, not compulsory but a voluntary lecture. I mean, I've done it – 520 secondary-school teachers in a large hall for two hours. You can get them up and doing something, but is it meaningful? All they remember is – I think we did a bit of breathing. Because it's not internalised. You can't internalise something in a two-hour lecture. You can't internalise something in a whole year's lectures, can you? I mean, doing an MA in Voice, and it's difficult then, isn't it? But to expect somebody to perform at a professional level with two hours' training is... I can't even get my head round that as a thought. But it's ticking the box. You've ticked the box that says "Provide voice training".

B: I've always worked with the VCN, and I think that when you make contact – I worked with a school in Lambeth recently, and I was quite pushy inasmuch as how much I felt I needed to do. In other words, there is almost a point where you're going to get so little time that it could almost be destructive. So I pushed for quite a lot more than they originally offered. I pushed for considerably more. And they gave it to me. So I do think that it's worth always pushing for that bit more, explaining why you need to. If you've already got a teacher, or whoever is in charge of NQTs, or if it's university, who's in charge of training there – if they're talking to you they're already sort of onside – you can push it a lot further. I would encourage all of us to try and be a little more sure of ourselves, and even slightly more evangelical about what we need to do. Also, which is very important to the VCN, with teachers, is the vocal health issue. It's all about that, and as employers they have responsibilities with regard to those issues.

A: So would it be fair again to say that what's being proposed is that it's not just a question of carrying the subject voice into the zones of study that students are going through, but it is somehow or other altering the complexion of understanding about what voice is, and how it impacts on education across the board?

VARIOUS: Yes, absolutely. It's a culture change.

L: I've introduced into my work as a freelance, what we call "twilight sessions". I now do six to eight sessions after school over a period of possibly two months, depending on how we can fit it in. So that people have time to go away... You've introduced them to some idea about the voice, and then they can go away and they can practise that. I think the one thing that is missing... I know that Ros Steen was talking this morning about... she doesn't teach breathing, she goes with the person. To some extent that's fine, but a lot of these people don't know what a voice is, they don't know how it works. They're all breathing upside down and they're all standing badly, or they'll sort of lean on a table and expect the voice to work, so they don't know anything about posture either. It's all those things. If you're putting those back together in the right way, and making them understand that by doing that, actually, you feel better; by breathing a bit differently, that makes a change and the voice gets bigger – then you've got classroom control. Because the big thing that they're all worried about is classroom control, nothing else – it's about behaviour management. And if you can say to them: this is actually going to improve your behaviour management by 130%, they come with you. And then they try it out and it works, because the voice is now saying: "I'm in control, and I'm in control of you, and therefore you're going to do what I ask you to do." But if I go in with a slightly querulous voice that's not really working, and I say: *[in a high-pitched, quavery tone]* "Will you all sit down, please?" Even at university level, that's not going to cut the mustard either, because the voice says: "I'm not in control of myself; therefore I'm not in control of you". And they say: "Well, who the hell are you, then?" And then you get problems.

C: Another model that I've found really works is to try and encourage the school or college to have you go in and observe. That is so valuable, if you can sew that into the training. The observation, even if it's just half an hour, even if it's for 10 minutes, you can see if the posture is not working – you know what it's like – that makes a massive difference. Then, if you can possibly sew in a one-to-one with that person, post-observation, so you get the school to timetable a bit of time after the observation. Then they come to the twilight session, and they get the whole thing. The big thing about working with teachers is that they're so stressed. Particularly newly qualified teachers are unbelievably stressed, and almost unable to listen any more. So you have to find ways in with them, and take time. They're one of the most difficult groups to teach voice to. But what I would suggest as a voice teacher is that you learn so much through working with a teacher, not only about their different issues – you're also, in a way, looking into a mirror-image of yourself. So as a voice teacher you learn an awful lot about the voice by working with teachers.

G: Have we defined the difference, then, in terms of the work of an HE or FE lecturer versus the teacher? Because I'm wondering if we need to look at that a bit more as well, because we were talking about behaviour management, and I think that's a very different issue post-16, post-18.

L: At FE level, 16-18, there are issues of behaviour. I think even at HE level – because I've taught in HE as well – that it's not entirely unknown that students do not necessarily do what they're told to do, or want to do what they're told to do. But there isn't a lot of difference vocally, I would have said, in all those situations. I was only mentioning behaviour management because that is the real issue, obviously, in primary and secondary education, but I think it's creeping in a bit further up as well. A lot of lecturers are concerned about behaviour… students talk all the time and don't listen to what's being said. That sort of thing. It may not be the sort of behaviour management you've got in a secondary class, where they're actually hitting each other sometimes, as I saw in a class the other day. But it's this constant talking, and not listening, that sort of thing, whereas that wasn't happening 25 years ago.

C: One observation I've made, because I've been teaching at drama school for three or four years and now I'm teaching at a university, and there is a great degree of flexibility to change things with voice. Brunel have seized what we've been doing over the last term and are more than quadrupling the amount of hours that will be dedicated to the students, but it's simply because the students have the ability within the university to dictate their interests. They can sort of create – my head of faculty was interested in the feedback she was getting, and she said: it's entirely up to the kids if they want more. That's something you often forget, that actually the kids in university can, just through sheer numbers and desire, change things. And that's what they've done, which is something that I think a lot of us just think, oh well, we're teaching there that morning…. But actually you can change things, and stretch voice, so that it becomes much bigger, much more important. These are not performers, they're mostly going to write or be directors, but they're that interested in the voice. All I wanted to say was that you mustn't forget this idea of flexibility within the university system, because you can mould and change and be evangelical within the university.

O: I've just graduated from AT, I went to university. I understand what you're saying, but at the same time it's important to say that sometimes a lot of people are going into AT and they don't know what voice is. So you're up against a back wall straightaway as soon as you go into somewhere like that. When I first started university, I didn't have a clue. I would say that out of a group of thirty-two of us, there were three of us who took any interest in it.

C: What was your subject?

O: Drama and community arts. But you need the support of the other lecturers around the voice lecturer to be telling you that it's important. Otherwise it looks as though the voice teacher, battling away, doing their own thing, which is completely devoid of everything else that's going on in the course. So it comes back, almost, to the teachers and the lecturers. You need those lecturers to be also saying to the students: "Your voice work is as important as your movement classes or your acting classes" or whatever. Sometimes in higher education – certainly in my establishment – that wasn't what happened. They didn't care what happened in voice class, as long as you were having it.

C: Cross-fertilisation is very important, which my head of faculty has created. She is very keen to bring voice to all other parts of the university, which is such a huge... you know, there is every subject under the sun. If we're going to change voice, if we're going to not have those responses you had in your vox pops, that would be the first thing: to be evangelical, really. Every time you go into a different work situation, to think sideways, laterally. To think: "I'm here with these people but how..." You know, push it. Change it.

G: I would agree with that. Going back to this idea of what you're saying, I think, about working with the lecturers' outcomes. What do they actually want, what do they want to achieve with those students? What is the whole point of their lecture or their subject area, and in what way are they going to reach the hearts and minds of their students? And once you've actually got that, then they're beginning to think laterally about, well, how do I actually motivate and move those students, get them actively engaged in what I'm doing? When they realise that voice is a significant part of that, then they might take more action, because obviously if you're a maths or geography teacher or somebody that doesn't think very much about the actual delivery of your text – I'm using the example of somebody who may not be terribly alive. An ex-colleague of mine used to talk about "delivering audible print". I think it's a wonderful expression. You know, text in your hand, goes into your brain, goes out of your mouth – there is no connection at all. Whilst someone actually sinks down to a much more visceral level. I think once they realise that... Again, as mentioned this morning, it's something about not just standing up in front of people and imparting knowledge, that actually that's not the job any more and the lecturer's job isn't just to be...

L: We should be asking the question: "What is voice for?" and not "What is a voice teacher for?"

G: And how does voice serve the context? Because I think we can talk about voice and then worry about why people aren't thinking about voice, but we're actually not going into their mind-sets and their belief systems about what they're trying to do, and the only way we're going to actually get them to teach is... we've got to work their language.

L: Exactly. But we've got to make them understand that what they are saying... I mean, I work with teachers a lot, and if you talk to teachers and say "Who inspired you to be a teacher?" it was another teacher. When you ask "Why was that teacher inspiring?" it was often the way they taught and the way they spoke. That becomes the hub of it. We've got to inspire people and inspire each other. We haven't got inspiring people. They may be inspired, but somehow they can't be inspiring, if that makes sense.

H: I was just thinking about the cultural context – it's a large generalisation – in which most universities and higher education operates, and corporate as well. It's very much the value set which has dominated the world for the last five-hundred years, which is that of: "We can use our logic and reason to control society, individuals and the natural world". It's a value system that is very much based in the head and is pretty disconnected from the heart and the gut. ... I think the big question is first of all, how can we create a space in which people working in higher education can begin to understand that by connecting, you've got healing – healing being "whole", a similar etymological root. That connecting to the emotions, to the heart, to the gut, to the physicality, to the tone... many lecturers relate to word, without the tone or the physicality. How is it that – by seeing presentation in all its manifestations as a performance art – can they raise their ability to connect, and also move away from being obsessed with their own "How can I be interesting?" to "How can I be interested in what's going on out there?" Because the value sets of many of their students are the same as their own. And it's that need to be flexible and adaptable, and to connect out there, that is the big shift that has to be made.

P: What E said; I totally agree with you about this five-hundred years of, you could say, "anti-body" thing, Christianity and rationality... . And in a way the IT world is like the logical extreme of that: everything has gone up here into the eyes and into the brain. And those recorded, digital voices that are replacing our living voices are like the extension of that to the most absurd degree. What you said about "not only the beautiful voice" – that was my introduction to voice, really, the first voice lessons I had in 1967 with one of Roy Hart's first students. She was one of four people who were allowed to teach after working with him for about five or six years. This thing of long experience and training before you teach others, even. It was not how to sing, it was how to actually express all the anger that I had in me, but do it on a note. This was part of Wolfson's genius, to hold that note but to bring the energy of the repressed emotion into the sound. Such a liberating thing at the end of that hour each week, I felt: here I am, this is who I am. It's not all that other stuff that had been driving me crazy for months and months.

And now, forty years on, I have an experience with higher education in the last two years, attempting to get a research fellowship at the University of Central Lancashire, which a couple of people in the performing arts department there had encouraged me to do. They wanted me to come in and work for three years to bring voice, Roy Hart voice into the department. My proposition was that working on this level of sound, making bridge between person and performer, could create a connecting feel between people in different disciplines: those who'd come to dance, those who'd come to work in theatre, those who'd come to work in music and technology, which as it stands, they come and do their sessions, they have no space where they meet other than in creating little productions. But they don't have a basic understanding of this creative medium that is sound, the basic sound of the human being. I put a load of work into it, and so did other people. Twice it got turned down for the most fatuous of intellectual reasons to do with criticisms about the way it was put on paper and proposed. So very frustrating, and they were all upset, and I was upset. The attempt to get something of this Wolfson research into higher education – you've got to be evangelical, yes, you've got to be even... I don't know what it is that it needs to say: "Hey! Look! Here's some stuff that's just been waiting for 50 years!" You know, Roy Hart had to leave. Peter Brook had to leave. People left the UK 40 or 50 years ago because it was as it was.

B: Are we saying that, in fact, we're leaving higher education out of the equation because we feel that there has been this dangerous period, and that all the people who are going through higher education at the moment are stuck in this maelstrom, and maybe somewhere out of it all will come something more worthwhile to be achieved? It could happen like that, but I do suggest that somebody has to instigate. Somebody has to go in and proselytise. And within higher education particularly, and I'm talking now about universities rather than further education, about which I know nothing, but universities themselves – each have their own authority to do what they like. The only thing that's brought to bear on them to do stronger things is when they're being offered money in a specific way, like from the Higher Education Funding Council, who have now said that anybody who's going to do a PhD, if they are being funded by the Higher Education Funding Council, which doesn't mean everyone who's doing PhDs or MAs, must do two weeks' training. That is then left to each university's training officer to decide who they are going to call in, first of all, to get a few external people. And then, usually because it's cheaper for them to do it – the training officer will say, "Oh, they get voice sessions, we went to a voice session. OK, we could do voice. Oh yes, somebody came in and did presentation skills, we can do that." It becomes in-house. Again, you have that little window of opportunity: tick! With the students coming up now who are actually being more market-driven and making universities take notice of them, and with the idea as well, which has to be said, that to teach in a university is thought definitely infra-D – it's our research that's so important. Please...teaching informs research: we know that, don't we? We've got a student in front of us who wants to learn something about voice – they immediately become our method. You don't think: "Oh, I know how to do this!" You think: "What have you got? What can I help you with?" All of that has got to be changed within the culture.

C: I'm very lucky because I've got a very sympathetic head of faculty. I was thrown the gauntlet. The voice subject was failing, and it was one module, and I said it was very difficult to teach – I'm frightened to go in for one term. So I said: "Well, look, I'll just teach them how to warm up. That'll be enough. That'll take a term." But during the course... it seems to me we're talking about drama schools and higher education in terms of teaching drama. What I've found – the big contrast is that, my experience in drama schools is that they're white middle-class, and universities most definitely are not. And our subject lives with that type of mixture. It just makes the most extraordinary, exciting thing. Because you have 21st century English society there in front of you, instead of a more rarefied form or strata of society that you get at drama schools.

I: I've been sort of feeling on the outside of this, because I'm working in the American system, where there is voice teaching for everybody. I didn't quite appreciate that until I heard you describe two hours, for a teacher. In three universities where I teach, and in fact in every single university in the United States of America, every student must take at least one full term of voice work. It can be called Fundamentals of Speech, Voice and Speech,

Presentational Speaking, Professional Business Presentations, Effective Presentational Speaking – call it whatever they like, it's voice and speech, and particularly if it's taught by a voice teacher. How can I describe it? It's a very interesting comparison, because they have to take it. How it came about, I'm not sure. How long it's been there, I'm not sure. But it's a tradition, and every single undergraduate student must take a full semester of voice work. What happens is that they go: "Oh, gosh!" They have several required programmes. And as one of their required programmes they're a little afraid – still, they feel it may be of more value than some of the other things they're required to do, but they wouldn't necessarily ever take this subject of their own volition. And yet, having taken it, they vote it consistently among their top favourite courses at the university.

So the result is – nowadays American universities are incredibly customer-driven – so you have more voice if they like more voice. It's an interesting – because it's sort of beginning to work here in that way, too. It's starting. So I really take on board this business of, if you introduce it to the student somehow, and the student likes it, then it happens. The result is, however they find them – and they require at least an MA qualification to teach the subject, so they've got to find teachers who at least have a Masters degree in a subject, not a related subject, but something that's essentially voice or speech – and they find them. They must have tens of thousands of voice teachers who are meeting this requirement. Where they train or where they find them, I don't know. But it's such a different experience that I'm finding it very hard to relate with all of this that's happening, because this is truly voice teaching for everybody. It works so well that I wonder why on earth the United Kingdom, in an age when these oral skills are more necessary and viewed as more necessary by both students and society in general – why we here would find it so difficult to introduce. That's why, when you talk about evangelism, that's what I feel. It's not a matter of being nice to these lecturers and give them a little extra hour.

It's "get in there and insist" or show in whatever way you can that this works, and that students want this when they taste this, and it brings in money. Whatever way we need to sell it, it certainly works in other scenarios, and it's well worth our looking over our shoulder at what other people have been doing for generations.

G: We're reluctant to take anything that's American. I lived in the States for eight years and taught in the HE sector over there, and you do have to take speech communication, which is what we called it at San Diego State University. You had to take freshman composition writing, you had to take maths. It is about rounding out people. Obviously at British universities, they would call us very elitist, because it's about only certain people with certain qualifications are allowed to get in, so you deny entry. So already we're going back to that split that you'd mentioned earlier, about particular types of people that might be allowed in, and also dealing with the Cartesian split, which is that mind is more important than body or emotion, if you think about it. So in Britain you've got a system that values specialisation, elitism, intellectualism above everything else. It's no wonder that voice doesn't feature, actually. And you're talking about something that's actually more mystic.

A: One thing I would say is that, as a body of professionals, I suspect nothing will happen unless we find a way of having a common identity, a common voice. Unless we do that, this is just going to roll on, in actual fact. And it seems to me that the forces that are impacting upon education – be it conservatoire, university, HE college or FE college, whatever – the forces that are acting upon them are very, very, very strong. We are seeing changes now within the canon of drama schools that exist in this country... I do know that a lot of debate within the drama school sector about "How do we find the resources?" and "How do we honour learning methodologies that actually do a proper job, insofar as training the voice is concerned?" How do you set modules – if you've now got to go up the module root because you're having to make liaison with universities, and so forth – how do you get modules to actually respond to the whole person? Is it possible? And so on. So there is a lot to be done, and it won't happen unless we have more dialogue with each other. A similar thing such as this, for example, next year.

We have to know our subject as well, across so many different directions, so that we can keep retuning the technicalities that underpin us, so that we can interpret, interpret, interpret with whoever it is that we're working with, so that we can encourage them to write their learning in the book of their body, in the book of their life, so to speak. Which means that we – they've put a lot of pressure on power training, on the way that we're serviced by the institutions where we work, they put a lot of pressure on whether we're dialoguing with each other or not, and also a huge demand on our need to get out there and make sure that people do know what it is that we do and what the subject is about.

Chapter 7
Voice in the Community
Excerpts from the Discussion

Chaired by John Wild. Discussion Brief: Who needs voice training? Who gets it? Whose voice are we teaching? How does voice training connect to the wider community in terms of disability, ethnic heritage, business, youth/prison work, class, gender, etc? How do we address the teaching strategies needed to deliver appropriate training for students from a multi-diverse community?

The excerpts are quoted but not named – people are given letters A-Z. A is John Wild, the Chair. Z is a person unidentifiable from the recording.

A: I suggested this morning that we'd use the "who, where, what, when, why and how". We start with the who. Who do we think we're dealing with? Where are we dealing with them? Why? I don't want to impose any of the ideas that we shared this morning. So if anyone wants to kick off: who do we think we're dealing with here?

J: I've been working with somebody who is an immigrant, who's been in this country for about six years, and has never got over the initial shock of arriving in this country, being foreign, and finding that everybody else is speaking a different language to hers. She was well taught in English at school in her own country, but that nevertheless didn't reduce the trauma of her initial arrival. She's full of negative self-perceptions about her speech now – not that her speech is nearly as bad as she thinks it is – but just because this initial trauma is still with her. So in a sense maybe there is a sort of paradigm there for a lot of people in the community at large, where a heritage of negative experiences of that speech lingers on… the negative experience was arriving here as an immigrant – I don't know the circumstances that brought her here. She'd at that point have been around the age of 19 or 20. And just coping with that, and having to start a new life in a foreign country in a different language community. I'm trying to reconcile her to her voice and to her speech. That would be the subject of what I'm doing.

K: In terms of private lessons, I've worked with young trainee barristers who were second-language English, who were very keen to do RP to be taken more seriously in the workplace. I once had a barrister who did a lot work in the Caribbean in quite a small room, which kind of puzzled me, and he said, "No, the reason is that the fans are going all the time and I need to be heard above the fan." It seems to be all very specific – whoever perceives they have a need. On that, I often would ask people; "What do you think you need vocally?" and very often they would put their finger on it straightaway. I often like to do a diagnostic, but when they've said what they've said, I would usually agree with – which is another interesting thing about self-diagnosis. People are often right about what they think they need in vocal terms.

C: One of the things I'd say in response to that, and also from the film we watched – the vox pop – it's not so much "it's whoever thinks they need us". It's "they don't perhaps know they need us", because nobody knows what a voice teacher does. There is something about a lack of knowledge about who we are and where we are; I think there is lack of places to be employed, because that's endemic. It's not just individuals, it's institutions. And finally, I'd ask the question: "Who can afford us?" Because, you know, this is our job and we need to make a living. And if we're not recognised, if no-one is paying for it on any level, even if people recognise they need it, then there is a very narrow segment of the population who can actually afford it.

E: Something we were talking about this morning in "Voice and Higher Education", which is something that fascinates me, if you go back to 1959 – I was looking in the archive – there is a whole set of articles on Gwyneth Thurburn training teachers at Central, training them in posture, voice, breath and resonance to quite a detailed level. That's a level that only actors reach, really, now. At that point teachers were doing it. Now, I understand it was a different world, and that many voice/speech teachers were teaching things that are no longer relevant. However, why is it that a teacher in 1959 had access to a good, detailed, sound voice training? They need it now more than ever, because children are so much less disciplined. They're not getting it. There is very little voice training for anybody other than actors. Why have we gone backwards? That's what I don't understand.

L: The irony is that when people are promoted, very often they are promoted into a situation where they have to do more public speaking and control groups, as it were – they use those words "chair events" – and it has nothing to do with their field, they could be a chemist or a meteorologist, and now suddenly they're not a chemist or meteorologist, they're actually a public speaker. If there is some way we could get that information across to businesses: that they have to, immediately upon promoting someone, that's part of the re-education they have to give them. Because those are the kind of people who come round. It's very often men or women around the age of 30 or 40 who are really going from feeling themselves "young people" – junior members of their society and profession – to suddenly senior members, and they're not ready for it. They're not vocally ready. They come in saying "I want gravitas in my voice", "I want people to believe me."

B: ...if people knew we were there, they would want us. Because I get extraordinary people phoning me up and wanting help, and they really need help. I get the middle-class lady who's working as a translator at home all day, and she rings me up and says: "You're a voice teacher, can I come and see you?" And she comes to see me, and basically she's stuck all day with her computer, and everybody around her tells her that she's a bad communicator. There are so many people who want me for different reasons. I get a lot of foreigners with their problems, as you know, which can be vocal or social or psychological or whatever. I just can't tell you how many different people want you for different reasons. Sometimes, you know, you just have to see them once or twice. It's like going to a tennis coach: all they have to tell you is to throw the ball higher in the air and you can serve, and you go: "Oh, is that all it is?" So you just have one person, you say: "Why aren't you breathing?" You don't have to tell them how to breathe, they know what you're saying.

So I just think the money is there, somehow. When I think that people pay for people to walk you round Clapham Common as a sports coach or something, I think surely you can ask the same amount of money for giving them something far more valuable. Or you pay people to tell you what to eat. And we're asking people to pay us to communicate, to open yourselves up, to express yourselves. There is a lot of work out there, even vis-à-vis schools and things. Luckily there are now quite a lot of people helping teachers in schools. It's just that unfortunately it's not everywhere, as you know. But the great thing is that everyone's so enthusiastic about it. This is why I don't feel we need to be downcast about it, because the people out there actually do want what we have to give them.

E: For me, if I have to explain to someone really what I'm doing, it's about allowing them to find a way to be more confident in a specific situation where they're not.

K: Sometimes you also think people get more confident when they have a more comfortable voice, so you might be working to get their confidence by working technically on the voice to give them confidence. But sometimes the problem with the voice is lack of confidence anyway – so it's sort of a circular thing.

L: We have gone through, though, quite a sea change in terms of even the word "enunciation". I remember my auntie, who was born in 1906 in America, used to have to speak poems out loud in school, and had to have public speaking, and even I had to have a public speaking class, and that was all part of the curriculum. But then it became posh – you know what I mean, we have been tainted with that word. I don't think we've reinvented our public image yet as something deeper and more profound. It still is: "Well, they'll teach me how to speak properly so I'll walk around talking like that." Even the actors, after six months, sometimes ask: "What are you doing? That's not about speech! That's not what we want."

H: I think it depends how much we have had to put ourselves on the line for what it is we believe in. It's all the same, whether we direct actors or people in the commercial or whoever it is, I think it's about examining yourself and yourself in relation to others and the community and the world, and what you believe in. As voice teachers, I think that in a way it's branding and how you want to use the language to describe whatever person or community that you're working with, whether it's an acting community or whether it's schoolteachers. The language that you use is part of it. At what point do you introduce Shakespeare to prisoners, because it's an incredibly empowering battle scene where the language sounds invigorating and empowering, without saying that it's Shakespeare?

C: One of the most exciting things I've been doing in the last year is working on developing a pilot project for people with multiple and profound complex disability, and working to bring them into the umbrella of an educational system, in a pre-entry level curriculum strand of communication. I've been working quite closely with speech and language therapists to develop a dialogue, a common ground and common understanding of how to give and develop voice to people whose voices quite literally are a grunt, and bring it out and develop their means of being a valid person within a social context. For me, it's drawing on every resource I've ever had in my life. Just really recognising the need for this reaching out and working with a speech and language therapist, because they have a background I don't.

I'm starting to recognise the need to reach out and establish connections with everyone in the field, because it's not one thing I can do on my own. I've had speech and language therapists start sending clients to me, because they see I do things that they haven't had the discipline or the training in their discipline… . It's very much a process in the wider scale of things about who are we and what are we doing, and how do we make that available to other people? I think it is very much a changing social situation that we're in. I've been doing a lot of training myself within community arts, and you'd think in music faculties they'd offer voice training, but it's not there. At a very limited level they will do singing and repertoire, but they don't do voice production. Why not?

L: I think there is a commonly held belief that when you open your mouth to speak, you don't set muscles by choice. You've set muscles and that's it, you can't change it. But I think probably for me at some very late date recently, a very famous voice teacher said to an actor: "Well, you know that before you speak you set muscles. So you could set them differently." She didn't say that in a patronising way, but it was quite fascinating, and I thought, oh my goodness, that's true! Of course it's true. But I don't think the average person believes that. I don't think they conceive how we can help them, quite quickly really (as somebody said), to make that choice. Because you get to a certain place in your life… Maybe your father told you when you were a little girl that *[raising pitch]* you really had to speak like this to be loved, or that *[dropping pitch]* you had to do that as a man. And you could make that choice differently when you got to be 30 or 40 years old.

J: And it can be a very joyous moment when somebody discovers that, discovers that those choices are available.

F: I was 20 years old when I went to France, and I didn't speak the language. I just felt that getting accepted to the school of my choice was enough. I'm sure you all know about France, there is the familiar and the formal. To listen and to learn the language, and never really having the confidence that I am in the language, I am communicating in that language that is not mine. So in a sense if I were faced with someone, I would take this personal experience of this never truly knowing, never truly being within that language fully – take that experience and somehow use it as a tool to empathise with this moment of her trauma. I spoke earlier today about the physical American "let's get out there and do it" attitude, and perhaps somehow within my nature I just forge ahead and it doesn't matter. But using my own personal experience as a tool to interpret to identify where it is that I should approach this particular issue with a student. And you're right, it is therapy.

F: …being here, I'm amazed: I can say two words to someone and they'll say: "Where in America are you from?" I don't feel categorised in that sense, I'm just amazed at how acute the listening capacity is here, and how fine it is. In America, we have dialects and accents, but there is so much more space in between each one. Here it's all condensed, and you're all on top of each other, very closely… . One beautiful image: the accent if you're within the sound of the bells, you have, what, the Cockney accent, is it? What an incredible image! To just have an accent that is within sound waves. It's amazing to me, just amazing. Of course we're talking about a much greater space in the United States.

Z: …it's about listening to who it is that we're working with or teaching, as well as offering them what we've got. A girl on our course was German, and she found that when she was speaking English, her voice was much higher, and so she felt disempowered and childlike. She only started finding her personality as a teacher – as a human, and as a teacher – when she was working in German. I'm also working with a young Nigerian girl at the moment, who, as well as opening up the vowels in a different way – literally the breath has got lower. Her voice, which was really breathy, is now this big voice, and she's having problems at home because her family are telling her off about it. So working with any community, the responsibility that comes with that is something to bear in mind. And it's not therapy, but of course it is, but it's not...

E: I find that a really interesting question, because I know that, at the moment, in East London, in Hackney and boroughs around there, is a big project by the LDA to bring particularly Bangladeshi and Eastern European women off benefits and into work, and specifically into entrepreneurial activities. Now, that point raises a Pandora's box of issues, doesn't it? Because in order for these women to achieve an entrepreneurial activity, they're going to have to develop certain vocal, physical skills that currently they're not employing. When they then take that back to husbands and children and traditional communities, that's a fascinating time to be around, isn't it? Because that's a huge shift. Very, very interesting question. And how much responsibility do we have, taking people from our model into... They've got to take on our model in order to achieve success in the workplace, but the model they are living in, in terms of families, is equally valid. Who's right? I don't know.

K: As voice teachers, you're wanting to give them the right voice for their body, which culturally may not have been allowed them, so you do that – and then you're creating cultural conflict.

B: I've had experiences in therapy work where similar issues have been broached, doing play therapy with cultures that do not play with their children, and explaining to them that this is what we could offer, but also to apologise for our ignorance of their cultures, and that no offence is ever meant, and then to take what's useful to them, but this is what we could offer them. It is really interesting when the two do collide, because you're doing the work with them for a reason, but it does often counteract it by causing offence. But if you go in there, open, saying, "I totally apologise for my ignorance if this does cause offence", then it opens up... you're not going in and saying, "This is how you should do it". It's just showing you're mindful, I suppose.

E: Having said that, they are being asked to go into work, and as liberal as my politics are, if they're being asked to go into, for example, banking or accountancy – currently very inflexible industries – it is going to have to be for them, to an extent, learning a choice that they can be employed in that environment.

D: It's a very difficult area. I live upstairs from a North London woman who has been in the Royal Free Hospital recently. She wouldn't eat – she's nearer 90 than 80 – she wouldn't eat if her lunch menu was taken by an African nurse, because she could not communicate with the African nurse. She could communicate with the Irish nurses. If you change the African nurse's way of communicating with the pensioner who lived downstairs from me, you might be affecting her home life. It's a massively difficult diplomatic exercise. I find accent reduction a very difficult diplomatic exercise. I was teaching one Serbian woman who couldn't be understood by her neighbours, and I taught her over quite a long period of time. And it came to a point when suddenly she was starting to be short with me in classes. And I said, "Are you sure you want me to keep coming?" And she said, "Do you know, there are certain vowel sounds I really want to hang onto, because they're part of me." She now understands me, so I think that's the end of our thing, which I'd stumbled across. I wish I'd been more skilful in finding out where the line was. But then I have a PhD student who's Chinese, who has a viva voce coming. Talking about vowel sounds and empire and class and all those terrifying things that get raised with that phrase, he finds it very difficult to distinguish if the word starts with a "T" and ends with an "N" – "tun tun tun" [for] "tin-ten-tan" – he finds it very difficult to distinguish. Now, how's he going to get through his viva voce if he can't distinguish between those three sounds? And he's concerned to make that happen. So it's not just a question of imparting information, as Ros was saying earlier; it is that skill of being able to listen and have a conversation. And it's difficult.

L: I as an American found it difficult to immigrate from one country to another. The longer I live here the more I think I'm not learning, that I'm not part of the language, even though I can do all the things I do. So it is fascinating, the depth of a culture is so deep.

D: Can I just ask: considering you're head of voice at RADA, where do you feel shut out?

L: Oh, it isn't a question of being shut out. It's a question of shared childhoods, I suppose. Because I would imagine that in certain places in America I might be equally foreign. We all have foreign-ness, no matter where we are. But I think the act of immigration – I think you don't know the questions to ask. It's not that you don't know the answers; you don't know the questions. Whereas when you've grown up in a society, somehow, where you've spent your first twenty years… of course I came here to drama school when I was nineteen, in that building. It would have been easier had I stayed in England then, as a twenty-year-old, but then going back to America and coming in my mid-40s… . Doing things like buying anything, houses, anything – it's just quite difficult. But it actually helps with teaching. I don't know whether you're asking this question, if it doesn't relate, but it helps with teaching tremendously, because I don't know what the prejudicial mind does, in terms of judgement. In other words, if I sit in front of a student, as an actor I don't care whether they're from Essex or whether they're from Scotland or Wales. I don't have the judgement that says, "Oh, well, you're like that because you're from Yorkshire". They're all human beings and we have the task of going into this play. So this play is the thing that's important, not where you come from. You're just a human being. I think that does relate, because you really are talking about listening to just the human being and the task that they need to achieve, which is what you were saying.

I: In a way, I don't know how to describe it, but I think language and cultural backgrounds are almost in your bones, whereas England will also be exotic, foreign, for me. And it's like I'm putting something on, whereas my skin and bones, that's Swedish, whereas the rest… I will never, ever be completely integrated, I don't think. That's both quite freeing, but it's also quite… you feel quite separate in a way. In the last ten years I've seen a huge change in the attitudes towards categorising. I feel there has been a really positive shift. That might be because I've been involved in voice, and I meet lots of people who are like-minded and so on. I don't know why but I feel there is a different attitude today than there was 10 years ago when I came here.

C: I've been in London for sixteen years. I agree with you. Even just watching television, there has been a rise of the northern accent as valid, and we can all start to understand what they're talking about. There has also been a downgrading in the poshness of radio people. The BBC voice is now something more middle-of-the-road than it used to be. I think there is a cultural shift, but everywhere – certainly in Europe – is experiencing the most incredible influx of different cultures, and I think that's changing us profoundly. We're in the middle of it – I think it's very hard to read what's actually happening.

A: It's all under one umbrella, which is about language, listening, communication of our work – that's what I'm hearing – vocal immigration, a label I'm trying to give... it's like we're receiving so many new sounds, we are having to adapt very quickly to those challenges. How do we? Do we adapt, or are we already equipped to deal with these challenges?

E: When you look at the history of English, it is profoundly adaptable, isn't it? The Anglo-Saxons were facing exactly the same kind of thing.

Z: And lost! *[Laughter]*

E: So I have great faith that this is a very exciting time in terms of voice, because I think if we are able to articulate what we do – and perhaps there is something around how we do that in a world that isn't about elocution and voice, it is new, it's different... but it's not new. If Gwyneth Thurburn was doing it in 1959, it's not new – we just need to express it differently. I think if we do that, it's very exciting times, because there is so much change, there are so many different nationalities. People are much more aware of the need to speak now than they were ten years ago, because their jobs depend on it. As we were saying, when they move up, they have to be able to present. So I think it's very exciting.

A: So it's fair to say that we're talking about the realisation that it's a multicultural community. It's not Voice in the Community – we've actually been debating what the community is. We are having to direct ourselves... I'm still hearing language, for me: its world, its clarity. What about the voice? Voice in community? You work in therapy – it would be interesting to strip language away, and conversation, articulation, accents, because we spend most of our time (I do) with people breathing. Because you talked about breath. What about breath in the community? What voice?

M: I'm a student at Central in the Masters voice programme. This particularly interests me, because two summers ago I came and studied with Caroline Goyder at a course she was teaching for a week. I'm a television producer by training, and I just came over as a lark, thinking wouldn't that be fun to do Shakespeare, you know, no training... just the breath work alone had such a physiological impact on me that when I went back to the States, the ratings on my shows went up, my life got... I mean, it was... if you're going to market yourself to the business community, my productivity shot up. And I guess my confidence, but I was already pretty confident. The breath work alone had such a physiological change. It lowered my stress levels, it made my brain clearer. And then I thought, this is great, I want to do this for a living! Because you really can make a huge impact on the business community, both in terms of how people feel... I know that with lawyers – there is a company here where they have a very high turnover in their young lawyers, and one of the reasons is that stress is so great, and depression. Well, the breath work can alter all that. It seems that voice people, if they work just on breath in the business community, can sort of speak their language, in that this will improve the productivity of your workers.

C: I did a day intensive recently – I concentrated on the fundamentals of breathing. You sensibly can cover in a day to give somebody some useful tools to take away. Their comment was that they – they're facilitators, they work with business clients – they wanted to deliver in one hour's consultation the tool-kit for their clients. Obviously I couldn't deliver that to them in a day, but that's what, as business people facilitators, that's what they're looking for. That's their understanding of what voice work is and how deep it needs to go to deliver the goods, really. I found that disheartening, to say the least. It was an interesting experience, but once again I think there is that lack of understanding that I'm hearing all day.

A: You said the same thing earlier, didn't you, B? About the more simplistic instruction you were getting?

B: Yeah, but I think they're worthwhile. Yesterday at the Foreign Office there was a dear woman there, she was Scottish, and she was – certain things just had not occurred to her. It was just a question of... I kept saying, "Slow down, slow down". She was rushing. Somebody said to her: "Would you do this in your real life?" It's just giving them that permission to slow down, to take time, to therefore address yourself intelligently to your child before you take the phone call or whatever it is. ... I just think if you can give somebody an hour, or any amount of time, it's always worthwhile. Because there is always something you can help them with. But the more I do the teaching the more I realise you've got to be so careful about what you pick up and don't pick up. Again, teaching with foreigners... I'm teaching Hackney council housing people and I'm saying: "You're giving me nil eye contact, you should be doing..." And they then say to me: "Where I come from you're not allowed to look people in the eye, it's bad manners." And you think, oh shit, that's so basic, I should know that! So you have to pick that up. ...But one thing I just remembered that was interesting to me, and it says something good about RADA as well. I had a Spanish girl come to me to develop her accent. The Spanish, when they speak English at you, it's very aggressive, it's really hard to take. And I didn't like the student particularly. She came at me, the fact that she didn't feel that her English – and she spoke perfect English – but she felt that she wasn't communicating, etc., etc. And I again – fortunately, a lot of my stuff is always the same: "Slow down", you know, because she was going much too fast. Anyway, she went away. And she sent me an e-mail a couple of weeks later and she had been on a Shakespeare course at RADA. She said to me that by doing the Shakespearean pentameter, she had learnt to get into a completely different rhythm with her English, and for the first time ever she felt she was able to speak English in a better. When she asked somebody something she felt that she was getting the right response. And that was just because she changed the rhythm, because, as I say, before she used to sort of shout at you and demand things from you.

D: M seemed to be in a position of power as a television executive in the first place, and then she learnt something here and has taken it back, not as a peripheral person, but back in a position of power. Ros Steen was talking about something this morning where she seemed to be in a position of power to take voice work into the centre of the rehearsal room. I think our power position is a wee bit peripheral, which is why, is it not, that business executives would say, "Jolly good, but only any use to me if you can package it into one hour so I can flog it". Well, we need to be in the centre to have the impact that we're capable of having.

A: Should we be inside the community that we're working with, or outside looking in? Is it more beneficial to be someone like yourself, who comes to London working with the voice communities here to benefit them, or to be somebody who is a Cockney, working within that cultural space?

L: When people call round and they're looking for a voice coach, I will always phone them and say: what specifically? Talk to me. What do you want, who are you? So I can guide them towards one teacher or another that might be best for them.

D: The personal element is so important in teaching, particularly in voice teaching... between yourself and the client.

Z: But in a sense as a professional offering the help, aren't you at one level always out? And yet, taking your analogy, you're always in as well, if you're making that contact. But there is a sense as an expert, as a skill provider, that you are out. Even if the person is in the house next door to you, they're coming to you for voice skills because you've trained and got those skills.

Z: But then the boundaries get blurred a bit if you think that it's actually a conversation. Think about what Ros said about if you're teaching people who are more talented than you, then you mustn't bring them down to your level. And if you're teaching people from different cultures, well, you're not to know every cultural tradition, so they're teaching you. And the power thing: I think that's quite a dangerous word. Isn't it a weaving, rather than a stepping on stones?

Z: We're learning together all the time, I think, with our students. But on the other hand it is our job and not the students' job, to facilitate the learning – that's the thing.

F: You and M were talking about breathing, and that's where it doesn't matter how your muscles from here forward, it doesn't matter where you are. The breath facilitates so much in terms of the sound, literally, in your mouth. And as soon as sound is in your mouth, there is vibration and there's support, your accent will change. It will – no matter what accent you have. So that begins a change and often makes people really clear, just because they're connected to their breath and vibration.

E: ....the thing that I love about voice work is that everybody I work with has a diaphragm, and has ribs, and has a backbone! [Laughter] So you could work with someone from, you know, a Zulu! And they'd probably have a better diaphragm than I do, in fact I'm sure they do... but that we are in fact all so similar, I think that's what I love about voice work, that whatever the cultural differences, that we have the same instruments, and that is very exciting.

D: The work brings into being our common humanity.

L: Empathetic listening, I think, from a deep place, not a superficial, cultural place.

A: Cultural conflict is one of the things that you were talking about. Communication of our work seems to be the big topic. The listening skills attached to that and how we all have to learn to listen in a different way, and how we've been perceiving it. "Vocal immigration" was the term. Listening attitudes have changed, and addressing that delicate balance, because it's not just listening to a voice, it's often listening to a culture, listening to an individual on a one-to-one (and God help us if you're working with a huge group of mixed cultures). And London is becoming more culturally and vocally diverse by the minute, it seems. But it is a positive, exciting time for a voice teacher, because we can multiculturally learn to communicate – multicultural communication, if there is such a word. Simple choices we offer can make so much difference – a very nice point to make there. I think we forget that, because we did talk very densely, but the bottom line in relation to Voice in the Community is that we have to be able to communicate quite simply, find simple ways of doing that, learning to understand that they are teaching us, if you want to progress. And knowing that everyone has ribs!

Chapter 8

The Urban Voice

Excerpts from the Discussion

Chaired by Claudette Williams

Discussion brief: Is the Urban Voice taking over? What is the Urban Voice? Is it a real sound or a myth? Whose voice is it? Is it evolution or regression? How do we teach the Urban Voice? Can we teach the Urban Voice?

- We are missing a certain kind of rhythm and global interplay within youth culture, perhaps within our training. I think I've missed it. I was asked to work on a play of Roy Williams. I'd read the play and I thought I understood it. And I sat there and thought actually, no I don't. I do not understand this language. And yes, you have to refer to a slang dictionary to actually break down the text. What are they saying? I mean, I thought I was hip! Instead of saying yes, "Believe!" I was thinking, what is "believe"? What does that mean? How do I then take that within class and break it down within text. I have to now go and get a dictionary of slang to actually understand all the new words.

- I just wonder whether it's about the identity of the voice teacher, feeling that they're not at the centre of culture, or cultural change. There is a problematic relationship there. [...] Presumably there was a sort of displacement for you at that point: feeling "Oh fuck, I don't think I'm at the core of this!" I'd feel a bit shit myself. It would set up some issues for me, I think.

- Initially we try and get them to find their own voice within their own centre, and then moving after that centre to various other accents. Quite often we're fitting other people's accents onto an RP resonance model. That might not be wholly appropriate when you break down what their accent is, and that adaptations may need to be made. It's an area that does need to be looked into in quite a bit of detail.

- In every language in the world there is a pronouncing dictionary that every foreigner has to learn so that they can communicate with everybody in that country. Therefore surely the national dictionary is the one that one should be going on, and everything else is wonderful to learn, and is useful in its own way, but when it comes to globalisation - we were talking earlier about words being used in the wrong context now, so people don't understand what other people are saying.

- But who writes the dictionary? Where does that come from? Who are the models for that dictionary? If you look at Longmans and/or other pronouncing dictionaries now, of course the accent has changed. If you want to call it RP or standard English or whatever you want to call it - it changes. We have to acknowledge that change. I think it's loaded politically.

- Is our voice work multiethnic? And what might that mean?

- It comes back to the vowels. It comes back to that, and if you think about it, the start of the sound we make. When we move from something which is a hum into a vowel, we are starting from whatever is there, the cultural basis for that vowel. So I'd say that's the starting point of whether it's going to be tying in with that multiethnicity.

- So what is multiethnic voice work? Does it exist? Does it matter? At Central we are doing a play with four black students. Those students are saying to me: "I'm going to find this very difficult, because I've never done it before." The "it" being "playing from self". You say, OK, but I've been teaching voice from self. What is missing? "I've done my Russians, I've done my this, I can do those, I feel safe as the actor. Playing from my own cultural/historical background – I've never looked at." I'm working on an August Wilson play at the Tricycle, and there is no textual understanding of the forms that August Wilson is using, which are African, and there is no way to go and research this. So where is multiethnic training, and how are we equipping students from different backgrounds within this training?

- All drama schools are open to all cultures, obviously. In theory. In practice it's not quite the same. It's improving a lot, actually. But there are not that many yet.

- Coming back to the concept of the urban voice: what is so interesting about it is that you've got this group of terribly diverse teenagers who actually are all from completely different cultural backgrounds, and they're all borrowing from each other's cultural background to create this common language. In my experience, that's unique. I don't even know how you would classify them as a group, because they're not... they've become their own group, which is actually exclusive in a very interesting way, certainly in terms of – I feel it's recreated a generation gap that disappeared largely. They are being "the young", and we are excluded because we don't have the vocabulary to join in the dialogue, even though some of them might be from our cultural background. I think that's really interesting, and I air it because I don't know what to do about it.

- A lot of this goes back to what Ros was talking about this morning, which is listening. If we encourage listening in our trainee students, which surely is fundamental if we're training actors, because if you don't listen as an actor, you might as well not be on the stage – it's about dialogue. We get them to teach us. So if you've got one in a group who is Jamaican or Nigerian or Bengali or French, whatever – you listen to them, and they bring their experience into the group. If you create an environment, and this is surely what we want to do, an environment where you don't feel so isolated. Yes, if you are the only white person in the group, or the only black person in the group, you are of course going to feel a little bit isolated, but it's up to us as facilitators to use that. Hopefully these days we're rather more open to that.

- We're not meant to understand teenagers. That's the whole point. A teenager does not want a 40 or 50 year old to understand, they don't want their parents to understand.

- There are two separate issues here. One is the "secret society" speak, and one is the accent. It's a manifestation of much more that's going on, and a lot of it, let's face it, is to do with something that the majority of us did not have, and that's drugs. A hell of a lot of it is to do with drugs. We didn't have ecstasy... a lot of it was to do with wealth. You couldn't have that sort of thing, you had gin and that was about it, because you didn't have the money to buy it. Kids today have a lot of money.

- We should look at this new dialect that's coming out and see ways that we can accommodate this into our training, and helping people to find their identity within the collective. That needs to be happening with everybody, doesn't it? I know this is a particular group in society that perhaps has not been catered for, but in doing that we need to make sure that we're not actually then singling them out and making them feel different to an unhealthy degree. There is a difference between finding your own identity and standing out, because you still want to be part of your group whilst finding that.

- This is going to be contentious, I'm playing devil's advocate. Given that we are training in the British Isles, I'm training in London, in England, in English, should I expect to embrace all cultures, or should cultures who are coming to me expect to be trained in this culture?

- The difficulty is that the Arts Council... there is a report called the Eclipse Report, and it now will fund with theatre ...if the plays reflect the ethnicity of the area. It is now looking at training in the sense that our students are users. Are we giving them the resources?

Chapter 9

Ring Tone vs Vocal Tone
Excerpts from the Discussion

Chaired by Katerina Moraitis. Discussion brief: What is the relationship of voice with digital technology? Is digital mass media modifying our perceptions of reality? What are the implications for syllabus construction, teaching strategies, assessment and styles?

The excerpts are quoted but not named – people are given letters A-Z. A is Katerina Moraitis, the Chair. Z is a person unidentifiable from the recording.

A: What I'm going to find interesting about this afternoon is the fact that I don't really know a lot about ring tone vs. vocal tone, and the areas that we can go into. When we talk about voice in the new millennium, we really are going into the new millennium with this type of work, because technology – and digital technology specifically – is changing all the time. So I'm excited to hear what your points of view are, and what your experiences are of that.

H: One thing I've noticed recently is that on the internet, the opportunities for using voices are becoming much more common, and I think this is both a good thing and a bad thing. The rise in voice-operated internet phone is noticeable. There are a lot more opportunities for using voices, admittedly disembodied voices, but voices, over a computer line, which wasn't the case even a few years ago. The internet has been dominated by typeface for so long, and now we're starting to see more and more voices being used over the medium, and I think this is likely to increase. Because after all speaking is a much faster way of communicating than... an internet chatroom, if you ever speak to someone by typing, it's a much slower medium, especially if you're communicating with somebody who doesn't happen to be able to touch-type. It can be a very slow process. There is a company who operate what is essentially a phone line over the internet, which is free for use and actually offers much better sound quality than a telephone. Where this leads us is what I'm curious about: whether this could be used – whether this could be seen as something that we as voice teachers could be very useful for, whether it's actually an emerging area for us to become interested in. Because as people start to relearn how to use their voices as a communicative medium over the internet, there may be more need for – or now an increased need for – input from voice teachers to help the communication, the communication skills.

A: ...this panel has been brought about by the need for voice teachers to discuss and find out what technology is going on and how we use it. It's not a new thing. As you probably know, in the 1700s there was a wooden (if you like) computer-generated voice that occurred by a man called von Kempelen,[1] and that was then taken further by Alexander Graham Bell, who, using the electronic tuning fork, tried to create speech sounds using the electronic medium. So it's not something that's fairly new in terms of not using the human voice and using the electronic or computer voice.

F: ...I can remember being asked back in 1991, by a major drama school, whether some of my courses could be done on CD-ROM – and that was then, 15 years ago! So listening to that, it brings that shadow up again, that it may be seen that some of our work could be done very comfortably via an internet site system, because you only have to put a camera on top of computers and so on. So that's something we might want to think about as a discussion, before we lose our hands-on, face-to-face, full-person teaching, if it's so much more effective. Accents, for example: it's so much easier without the person there.

D: One of the things that brought it home to me as a need to get tuned into, was several years ago, I had a connection with a set-up "broad ability" net, which was helping people with disabilities to get back into the workplace. One of the things which happened for a lot of them was that they had developed RSI in their hands from sitting at computers for lengthy times. So they were given voice-activated equipment, which was relatively new at that time, especially in a big usage. But of course then, without any voice help, voice tuition, they were developing RSI of the voice, if you like, because the actual wear and tear, and the work load, was so considerable – sitting for hours and hours at their computers – just the same as occurred with their hands as with their voices. This seemed to me to be an arena where we should be having a voice ourselves to say: if you're going to give people this equipment, you have to give them training as to how to take care of their voices so that they don't go the same way as other parts of the body and let them down. So that was my first connection with the impact of this kind of software.

C: The vocal expression has to be that much more precise when visual cues are limited – when you're looking at a small screen and the camera's in the back of the room. We get so much information visually, and that's not coming through as clearly. The onus is on the voice and its clarity and its specificity. And again, that's a place where our skills could and should be brought to bear if this medium is, at it seems to be, unstoppable, for better or for worse. There is a glaring need to make the voice more expressive.

H: Just to think on this issue of the possibility of tutoring over either telephone or internet or whatever technology you happen to be using: there is an innate problem with this, insofar as we're losing that personal contact, that ability to actually be close enough to someone to assess what needs, what kind of help they might need. On the other hand, given the rapid spread of the technology, it may be that we may find ourselves having to give accent classes over an internet wire or a telephone wire. I think we need to meet the challenge and we need to be ready for this kind of challenge to arise, because even if we make it clear – and I think we should make it clear – that there is no substitute for one-on-one personal teaching or even for being in the presence with a group, that type of teaching – it's no replacement for that. But at the same time that may be the environment in which we end up having to work.

E: My gut instinct, everything within my very soul goes: "We should resist this". You cannot replace the live teaching situation, the hands-on. Your perception changes once it goes through a microphone and technology, and you don't hear in the same way, etc.,

etc. The other side is that if we don't, if we aren't the teachers, somebody else will step in, maybe less able and less qualified, and there's the rub. I don't know the way out of that. It's frightening, actually.

H: One of my fellow students who was studying at the same time as me, one of the jobs he went on to do was giving voice training to people in Japan over the telephone… it was through a conference call. He had three people, I think, on the other end of the line. He was giving them instructions, exercises to go through. I hasten to add that he was not in favour of this, and he didn't like the results at all. But there is perceived to be a need, particularly overseas and particularly in Japan, where everything English. Everything that's done in the English language, is deemed to be so wonderful that people will pay a lot of money for it. And the friend of mine in particular, works through a presentation company, and this was the company that set him up to do this job. They thought, "Right, excellent! Voice coaching – we can do it using the technology, the Japanese will love the technology, so this is something we can really sell." Before he knew what was happening he found himself doing this job.

F: It's interesting, the question: what is a voice coach? We wear so many hats and have so many aspects. So whereas all my fears have been about: what do I do? – which is work with an individual's voice or whatever – I can suddenly see that if you're in Japan and you desperately want to practise your English, how wonderful, over the net, to be able to find a clear English speaker to have conversation with and deal with simple matters of pronunciation, which is a totally different area and I wouldn't have a problem with that. That's a really specific thing that has nothing to do with voice quality or connectedness or anything else, but simply about learning another language. So there are aspects, maybe, where it would be not a problem, but it would have to be so clearly defined as to what we were actually trying to achieve. You can see that would be a lifeline to somebody trying to learn a language, stuck somewhere, getting cheap and accessible – well, it may not be cheap – but accessible dialogue over the phone.

A: And whilst we're on teaching and training implications, what about things like singing or digital technology now, where the singer doesn't necessarily have to be connected, doesn't necessarily have to have a good voice, because digital technology can alter…?

E: …friends of mine who run a recording studio were explaining to me that the singer was a little flat in this phrase or over there, and they can change it. So this, arguably, is now not their performance that is being sold on the final CD. I'm trying to get my head around that. That's a moral issue, isn't it?

F: …everything in film is enhanced like that. The minute you take a performance and cut it the way you want to cut it, digitally enhance this, put in your CGIs and everything… we're constantly changing the world and it may bear no resemblance. That's why you can take an untrained person on film, because it's going to cost you more but you're going to do thirty takes, take the bit you like… . However, if you come back to really basic things – like if your actors do voices and whispers, no sound man can ever put a voice quality in there, unless they take it away and get someone else to do it in ADR [audio dialogue recording/replacement]. Because if it's a breathy and unconnected sound, you can't add tone. So you still need an actor to be using a connected voice, which so many of them don't. Something that came up this morning about perceptions of reality is that we seem to have got used to this total devoicing when we're listening or watching films. And even with the Big Brothers, which I don't watch, but people were saying it happens. In fact they still know they're being filmed, so it's not real. I actually don't think that's truthful, because in life you communicate. You have to be heard by the other person, or they're going to say, "What did you say?" And yet, when I watch so many films, the other character would not have heard any more than I can hear. And those same actors off-camera don't speak like that. They speak to be heard. So that's a weird thing that technology's doing.

A: ...it's that whole question of the TV or film or screen voice versus the actor, and the ongoing debate about how you train them – whether it's the same or whether it's different.

F: I think it is the same, except the only difference being that there is no audience, so you're absolutely not sharing, but you still have to have a good connected voice for the task in hand, however close that person is.

B: I would go further, and say an awful lot of it is about simple use of final consonants. For example, you will have a character in a detective story or something, where you have one person, where unless you try and lip-read them, you can't get what they're saying. Maybe I'm getting a little bit deaf, but I think it's an ongoing problem. I don't know whether it comes into this category, but I would say that it's huge, just simply not being able to understand what people are saying on programmes now.

F: I found myself slightly disagreeing with something that was said earlier today about how everything is changing, and acting is changing, and we have to change with, because I actually think that if you offer things that still follow those criteria of good grounded work and so on, people love it. They just aren't getting it. If you actually look at the people who I would say are working well in the modern field, and you look at the Johnny Depps or whatever, they actually do articulate. You can hear them. If you watch West Wing, you can hear – is it Martin Sheen who plays the president? – perfectly, it's the others you can't hear. So I'm not sure that it's true, I think it's just that directors aren't getting it. I had a director say to me recently, "I always ADR everything afterwards. I always ADR my whole films. I learnt to do it," he said, "because I get so much more focus in the sound, in the voice." I'm sorry, but that's because the actors aren't giving you the focus in the voice when you're shooting. That's why they have to go off to the ADR afterwards. So I don't think things are changing.

C: I find when people ask "What is a voice teacher?" they want to put it in the box of "stage": "Oh, so people can hear?" It's not *being heard*. I try to say to them, *being heard* isn't just about volume. *Being heard* is about the total communicative act. And that's where all this media – I guess it has been said – in a way it exposes more. The CGI creatures and cartoons relying more on the expressivity of the human. That wonderful actor who played Gollum made those films. In conjunction with all this technology, there is a need for what we do – even more so, because there is more exposed, the more refined these microphones become.

D: Well, I was going to say: the voice is the mirror of the soul. They lack the flow, they lack that other... whatever it is that we can't put our finger on, the spirituality, the essence of who we are. Being true to ourselves is one of the things that we need to be as teachers, and that we endeavour to enable the ones who we encounter in our teaching to be. I just think there is too much disembodied voice, even down to ringing up any kind of company and they're saying "Press one for this, press two for this," and then the whole series – you're just never speaking to real people, and it's gradually eroding something so precious and special. I don't know what the answer is, because I understand that it's here and we have to deal with it, but I do think that perhaps there is an argument for saying: "Hey, let's stop and look at this a bit more closely. What are we really doing?" Because people are not real any more.

H: I think we need to stress that the voice outside of technology needs to be developed and that there is no replacement for working with a teacher who can bring out that real essence to the voice that you were talking about. But at the same time I think it's important to keep in touch with the technology so that through the technology we can use that communication, the news reporting, the communication to hopefully let people know that this is necessary. Because I think there is a problem at the moment in that people, as we saw downstairs with the video, people don't know what the issues are. It needs to come from us – us as a body, maybe through the ICV or maybe some of the larger organisations such as VASTA or the BVA. We need to communicate to a broader range of people the importance of voice work. I would speculate that we can use technology to help us with that. Perhaps something like discussion sites via the internet. I know one of the ways in which voice use has been used in everyday life is for discussion; you have discussion groups – I know that there was one in the college that I went to, and I know that there are private discussion groups that people go to and practise discussing, practise speaking. Not a great number, but they're there. Maybe setting up a group via the internet that could use voice to discuss, rather than using an internet chatroom where you're having to type. What I'm thinking about is: how can we use the technology to inform the culture, in a way that is actually going to help? I don't think it's any replacement for learning how to use your voice fully and effectively in the way that we want to teach people, but I would hope there is a way of using the technology to communicate to people that this is an option.

F: Maybe people will find it – possibly this is being hopeful – but there is a lot of blogging, I believe, at the moment, where people do an awful lot of writing and so on, and loads and loads of people write their own poetry, and so on. So if that becomes spoken, and people are starting to speak poetry, and speak their thoughts, and so on, maybe in a weird way we'll end up with something more verbal...

C: I googled an old friend the other day, because I was bored at the computer, and found that she had done an oral history piece for National Public Radio in the States. And I found this whole website of archives of people telling stories that was wonderful. And it was wonderful to hear her voice over the internet. It was a great treasure-trove. I think another advantage of becoming more educated ourselves, more savvy, better able to work with these things, is that we're also then in a stronger position to draw lines in the sand and say: "I will help you work with this microphone in this situation, but I will not do it over the phone. I understand how this works, I understand how to work with it – it's not that I'm ignorant, it's not that I'm doing this and saying I don't want to be part of this – I do, I will, but there is a human element that I'm not going to sacrifice." And we're more able to do that the better we understand it.

F: That resource you were talking about with the stories and so on, the BBC have been doing their "Big Voices" thing. I had a lot of fun with time on my hands with broadband recently, doing that one… I wasn't terribly good at it, either, I was only sort of getting eight out of ten. You could test yourself. They would play accents and play things to you, they did languages and accents… but it must be a way of making people more aware of the whole scene, it's been a very good thing. They have also got this archive now of all these wonderful voices from everywhere, and they say: far from regional accents becoming more homogenised, on the contrary they're actually as strong as ever, dialectically as well as accent and phrases and so on. So that was an interesting find that they made. Maybe that's a part of the good way that the internet is making people more aware.

H: Given that voice over the internet is becoming more and more common, I'm sure that there are businesses and companies that would be very keen on building this up as an area. It's just a case of informing the right people in the right places. I was talking about Skype earlier. Skype run a free conference-call set-up, so you can include more than one person in the discussion. Now, I'm stepping a little beyond my technological know-how, but I'm fairly sure it would be a straightforward thing to set up a site dedicated to discussion, which could use Skype, in a similar way to Yahoo! Groups, which are basically like the blog sites you were mentioning, where people type reams and reams of information. A similar thing for voice discussion groups, for actual discussion groups, using the capability that the internet gives to access, to use the voice cheaply over the internet.

D: I had no idea that people looked, for example, at BBC Help Online as much as they do. And this Singing for the Brain project that I'm involved in, which was started by the West Berkshire Alzheimer's Society, which I lead now, and have been leading for two years, was written up by one of their science and health correspondents. It hit the internet at the end of November, and within days I found myself being quoted on the Bangladeshi Daily News… the message was clear, and the title was "Singing Unlocks the Brain". That has literally struck a chord with people, and the blogs that have come from that… . There have been masses and masses on so many different sites, lots of health sites, and yoga sites, and care homes… and that was, to me, quite a shock, because it's only in the last two years that I've become computer-friendly, had some lessons, got myself a little bit more au fait. And there it was I who doesn't deserve to be on the net, from what I've said about it in the past, was finding that this has really opened up a whole arena. We've had inquiries from all over the world about this training that we've been running. So in that sense, wonderful. But we wouldn't even dream of starting to do the training on the web.

A: When I go to Turkey, instead of hearing the calls to morning prayer done purely voice, you hear it over a microphone sent across Turkey or any Muslim country where they have any old calls that used to be done with the human voice are now done via machine. I think the same is… with film, in respect of actors are being replaced by blue screens. The recent film, for example, *Harry Potter and the Goblet of Fire*, was it called? Most of the acting was done with actors who weren't there, so technology has actually taken away the other actor and the reaction that an actor can have. I think as voice teachers, acting is one of our jobs. How would you respond to that line of our perception, or our actors', our students' perception of reality changing?

F: Even without the digital bit, there is always the danger of acting in a bubble in film, because you never have that ongoing rehearsal – you just turn up, and you've got your prepared performance if you're not careful, and there you are. So if you are actually then having to do it in front of the big blue screen on which something is going to appear, human or otherwise... . The film I've just done was almost all blue screen and with an actor who had never acted before. He had to react with this baby dragon and this bigger dragon...

B: I think it comes back to what we were saying earlier: this is a slicing up of everything into little compartments, which loses our natural flow, loses our real communication.

F: That's what has been lost, isn't it? You're right, communication... on the one hand we've got the reality shows taking over, so that you have this perception of reality as being this very mundane, underpowered kind of minutiae, but on the other hand the movies that are being made, and a lot of the other technology – modelling and so on – is going for digitising everything else so that you get more glamour, so that, as you say, you make the voice perfect, you make the body perfect, you use screens to make the scenery look perfect. So that everything is heightened and made totally beautiful, and on the other hand you've got the other side going on. It's fascinating. It's bizarre. We seem to need both at the moment. Or are we trying to take the mundane and transform it through technology to say: actually you're lives *are* glamorous, look! I don't know. It's a very strange phenomenon, reality TV.

H: That's the first time I think I've ever heard anyone put a positive spin on reality TV.

G: You don't have true photographs any more. Everything has been touched up. I think that's what it's all about: it's all superficiality and it's very rare that anything really gets down to its centre, to its core. That's what's missing and constantly needs to be addressed. You mentioned that we need emotion in communication, I think the business world has tapped into this now, only for the fact that – I don't know, maybe it was late 90s or something, I have no idea – it was faxing and e-mailing at that point, it was all about the written word. So what was lost with that was human voice and emotions, and things that were being read were being misconstrued. "I don't like his tone!" – and there wasn't any tone at all. They just might have perceived that he was being a bit cocky, "we're not going to do business with him" and that sort of thing. Now conference calling is becoming so popular because you do have that one-on-one communication. So you can't misconstrue the written word, you're having real people talking. You can see what sort of mood they're in, if you want to do business with them. That's why it's becoming more and more popular, and that's the way forward. People want to see each other, they want to talk and communicate, weigh each other up in business. If the voice teacher might move into anywhere, in terms of digital conferencing, maybe there is a field there: to come across the best way you can on screen.

B: ...in terms of teaching in drama schools, and you were saying about where young actors had to work with blue screen the whole time, and different levels and... we never teach that! We try and prepare them for everything, but all the things that you're talking about, about earthing, grounding... we should be teaching them how to talk, to act with thin air.

F: ...it is still your imagined reality and so on, but even more so, because of the blue screen and loads of technicians and... it's so much easier to just disconnect. So it is preparing people mentally for that challenge.

B: And giving them a self-reliance. We try and give them self-reliance in terms of preparing them for every eventuality, but it sounds as if, with all the different sorts of video technology, computers, etc. we have this animal that we need to create to survive in the world as an actor. It's becoming almost unrecognisable from even five years ago. It really makes you wonder what we're going to do next. We all try and bring in things like show reels, voice tapes, corporate role-play, all these things that you have to do in order to survive as an actor, but there is still a whole world here that we're not beginning to face.

H: ...is there scope for the voice coach to become more closely involved with the filmmaking process?

F: Ten years ago there were very, very few dialogue coaches or voice coaches, call them what you will, on movies. And now you very rarely see one that doesn't have, somewhere down by the tea boy, a voice coach or a dialogue coach. And that's because you're supplementing the lack of training usually.

H: ...there needs to be an educating of film directors. Film directors, from what I know, tend to come straight from film schools, where the emphasis is very much on the technology and on the process of making and editing film. I may be completely wrong here, but that's my perception of the industry. And I wonder whether we as a group, perhaps the ICV, BVA, VASTA, need to make some more of an effort to communicate to people working in film at the moment, maybe people who are training to work in film at the moment, people in the film schools – maybe we need to be a little more proactive in offering teaching to people who are currently training to be directors.

B: ...what we've been doing here is identifying areas in the digital world where voice might be used or we might have an influence, or we might be of use, or we might be able to set a trend... and I don't think we've exhausted them today. I don't know. I'm saying that out of ignorance. I don't think I know of all the ways it could be used. When you think of where recorded voices... and so when somebody gives you a telephone number, they've recorded a human voice, and they say: "The number is [robotic intonation] five-oh-three..." And then hearing an easyJet air stewardess, and I actually could see her sounding like a robot, and she didn't even have a script in front of her, she'd actually learned it in that voice. A lot of people don't know just how much we could help. So even in making those robotic voices you could get more vocal variety, you could get more range. I just feel very, very ignorant of what's possible.

F: We haven't even touched on the use of microphones in live theatre, which is going to happen more and more and more. Digitally enhanced voices in live performance.

A: Would you like to expand on that a little bit more, F?

F: Well, it's not really my field, but I know that even in opera now they have cleverly enhanced microphones. Especially in the West End, you will see more and more straight performances that are "helped", shall we say. And I think eventually audiences will say: why should we try to listen at all if it can be so easy to hear? And actors will perhaps not – because a lot of us are quite PC about the training, could I suggest, in a way... that why don't we have a generation of actors that you can hear all the time? When I worked at the RSC, we were having constant problems with young trained actors. And I work at

Regent's Park Open Air, and they're pretty good, a lot of them are still finding it really hard to "feel real" – we're back to the mechanical media – and use enough power that they can be heard comfortably. So you put those two things together: an audience who is used to digital technology and used to hearing very clearly at much greater levels than the human voice normally speaks at, and actors who are... because of that feeding in, "feeling unreal" going bigger... and perhaps as colleges like this become universities, cutting down on voice time and the amount of hours that an actor is going to spend training... . Then you put all those together and it seems to me that if we all come and sit here again in 25 years time that we'll find so much of it is miked? Which will lose such a lot.

B: It all becomes very bland, doesn't it? Very bland.

H: I think it's actually the one area of technology that does worry me. It really does worry about using mics in theatre, because it seems to me that theatre has for so long been the place where good spoken vocal technique has been guarded and where a lot of the big voices that are heard and are used on film have been trained and developed. That's where the big voices have developed. Much as it pains me to say it, I think that actually there is a certain amount of inevitability to what you've just said, F. It's very likely that we'll start to see more and more mics being used in theatre, simply because it's easier, and, as you say, audiences will expect it – expect not to have to work to hear what the actors are saying.

B: One of the most exciting parts of being a voice teacher in a drama school is the day when some of them "get it" about what they can do with their voices. They suddenly go; "Oh I didn't know I could sound so beautiful, I didn't know I could sound so rich, I didn't know I could sound so exciting!" Basically they're discovering resonance, and they're discovering their own bodies, they're discovering what beautiful sounds they can make. I think it would be so awful if, in the fact that people knew they were going to be miked, they would never find that out, that they would never have that time spent with them at drama school discovering. Because, again, when you see the more experienced actors on the telly, you can see them using their voices, or hear them using their voices to tremendous effect. Such power, such potential, such range. It would be awful if the baby went out with the bath water.

E: And also you are at the mercy of the aesthetic decisions of somebody in another place, who's got totally remote from the actual production, nothing to do with that. And I think also the general public who might buy a CD or a DVD or whatever it is, get used to that kind of bland wallpaper perfection, but when they're going to hear the real thing, they say: "But they didn't do it the same way as on my CD". I've got an old vinyl recording of Pablo Casals and three colleagues in the Beethoven House in Bonn, doing a Beethoven quartet. It starts with them tuning up and having a little chat. And you feel as though you're in the room with them. And they do make a few slips, actually! It was some sort of anniversary recording, and they were all in their 80s and 90s, these gentlemen, doing a wonderful, soulful performance. You would lose all that, because they could say: "Oh, they made a mistake there" – they wouldn't be listening to the wonder of rich older voices that people still go back to, and people who aren't with us any more – the Richard Burtons of this world, you know. That, I think, is the real danger, that we lose that.

C: On the hopeful side of the dwindling audiences for theatre, those people who do still go to non-tourist theatre go because of the specifically human experience they have there.

And if mics are introduced into those places, those theatres, to those audiences, I am hopeful that they will be rejected. Because people do go seeking something that isn't the movies, that isn't television. They can get, if they want, digitalised perfection... we can just hope that audiences will retain their sensitivity, that they'll know the difference, that they'll know the real thing when they see the real thing.

A: I think the good thing is that we're all sort of in agreement that it's the marriage of the electronic and the digital media, the age where we will be hearing voices through electronic media most of the time, even in the theatre, on television, on radio... there might come a time when we won't even be able to hear, for a while, a human voice spoken in that sort of medium. What I've heard is that there is a need for connection and grounding, and not less voice work but more voice work. Not traditional voice work, but a grounding in the voice work that needs to go alongside, parallel, working with technology. Some of the things that you talked about were fascinating about discussion groups on the internet, and actually using that technology to say, OK, if we're going to have to have it, then we're going to make use of it in a vocal way, hearing our friends overseas that we might be close to. Just being able to hear their voice through an electronic medium can touch us the same way a human voice can touch us without the electronic medium. Another point we made was educating directors, and educating those people who are in control of the electronic media, to say: the voice is not only important, it's the way that you communicate.

F: You were saying that we mustn't forget the positive, and talking to friends overseas. My friend has just moved to America, and where would I be without – we're just about to do Skype – without that easy access, you know, that I can just hear him like he was there, that I can e-mail him if I have a question. And any minute now we'll get our cameras up and see each other too. So there is a benefit too. When I left my parents in Africa to come here in '64, we couldn't even ring each other because it was £5 a minute, which is like £100 a minute now. So there are good things. It means we can be in touch with colleagues all over the world, that we can share ideas, that we can pool information. So I suppose if we take what's good and find a way of navigating what's destructive.

B: I think that's very important. Picking up from what you were saying, the isolation of work that can happen now, versus the community. I think we need to draw in those two forces together much more. And something we said about everybody wanting everything *now*. I noted this morning that Ros Steen said something about "Who's standing in front of me?" We have to have patience in the long aim, and maybe that's what we're also talking about. It's all relatively new, isn't it? It's going to take a long time before it actually comes together, and we can have harmony rather than discord. I'm very heartened by finding a group of people with similar views to me about the concerns this afternoon. It's lovely. And we've mentioned perfection quite a lot – everybody wants things to be perfect. But humanity isn't perfect. Wasn't it the Old Masters who often would put something quite incorrect and imperfect in their pictures to highlight the best of what they had? I think we have to remember that as human beings.

Chapter 10

Is The Dysfunctional Voice Becoming Commercial?
Excerpts from the Discussion

Chaired by Christina Shewell

Discussion brief: What is vocal dysfunction? How do we define it? Can it be achieved for commercial/artistic purposes? If so what are the implications for training? Should we be aiming to train vocal chameleons?

The excerpts are quoted but not named – people are given letters A-M. A is Christina Shewell, the Chair. Z is a person unidentifiable from the recording.

A: This morning's session is: Is the dysfunctional voice becoming commercial? What is vocal dysfunction? How do we define it? Can it be achieved for commercial or artistic purposes? Should it be? If so, what are the implications for training? Should we be aiming to train vocal chameleons? Now, I'm chairing this but I don't know what that first question means. So I want to throw that open: Is the dysfunctional voice becoming commercial? What do we mean by that?

F: I suggest it may be, because when I did the MA in Voice Studies, I took this as a topic. The fact that, like it or not, husky, slightly noduly, broken voices tend to be appealing to people. If you do research and you ask who people like, they like Mariella Frostrup or whatever, it tends to be when it doesn't disable the voice, perhaps because it mirrors in some way echoes of the sexual connotations of what happens to the vocal folds. It appears to be, at least in mechanical media, quite a desirable sound of huskiness. Obviously when you take that into a wider context of theatre, then you may have problems and you come up with the word "dysfunctional". In my field I find there's a desirability for a low voice, which may be produced dysfunctionally, a husky voice, and then we come on to the actors wanting to be breathy, but I think that's a different thing.

A: The question is referring to a quality, a quality suggesting dysfunction which may or may not be dysfunctional. So what are we going to go for? Or are we going to discuss them both? I think it's really important to define what dysfunctional means. Because when people do the voice training here at Central, it's a very small variant in voice that we're looking at, and we're saying: this is the desired voice, the optimal vocal function. That's the desired voice. And so voice teachers go out in the world with this perceived excellence, and perceived dysfunction is anything around that that doesn't meet that excellent quality.

Z: I do think that it is possible – and Christina would be the best judge of this – that some of the voices that are desired and perceived as desirable are, when analysed, caused by some dysfunction, i.e., a small nodule that the person's coping with and it's giving that particular quality. Not always, but quite often. And again you have to ask: at what point does it become dysfunction? Because it might be that taking away that dysfunction actually takes away part of that personality that one perceives as a really interesting voice.

Z: When I worked in Harley Street all those years solving voice problems, we always used to say that if Rod Stewart came in – which he never did – that we would never want to take Rod Stewart's huskiness away. We'd want healthy huskiness as opposed to unhealthy huskiness.

Z: And I've treated people like that who've chosen to keep their nodules, because it's got them work. So we've worked on healthy keeping of nodules. But they've chosen – they've had that conversation. They don't want it – it's getting them work at the end of the day.

Z: I think if someone suggested to Johnny Vegas that he change his voice, he would be very reluctant to do that. That to me is the epitome of the dysfunctional voice.

A: But of course if Johnny Vegas wants to do a show, six or seven shows a week, and his voice starts giving out, then he's going to have a dysfunctional voice – is that right? So the quality can sound dysfunctional, but if it's not causing problems to the person and it's not leading to long-term damage, we're OK about that?

Z: A larynx is not a fixed thing. Some people have a very robust larynx and other people don't, and that's what we're looking at – the person. You're not looking at: a larynx can do X, Y and Z. Some larynxes can do X, Y and Z, some can't do any of them, and some can just do Z. That's what we're really assessing when someone comes into a clinic. But what happens in a drama school is that often a voice teacher hears a voice – like the huskiness, the sort of thing we're talking about – and goes "Oh my goodness!". Lucky if then they can see a speech therapist, that's fine. But there are loads of people out there working with voices like that who are never going to be referred and never need to be referred.

Z: I went to a session run by some BBC casting directors in the summer, organised by South West Equity, and they were saying that they weren't interested in people who'd been trained and they weren't interested in people speaking with Received Pronunciation. It wasn't the actual physical dysfunctions, but the idea of – you were saying about training for a very small percentage, we were training people for classical work, and they're not going to get taken on, because actually what the commercial world is promoting is not trained work. So what we're hearing all the time is people who are not necessarily trained.

Z: If you turn on Radio Four in the middle of the morning, you can always tell whether you're listening to actors pretending to be natural people, or a natural person. And it raises the whole issue of the actor's voice. If we produce a voice that's too regular, does that actor then have the flexibility to go and play in EastEnders? Because actually vocal dysfunction is everywhere. There's a damaged voice, and there's a vocal dysfunction – and they're different things.

Z: There's the voice in training, where I do believe as a voice teacher I have a duty to make sure that that voice is in a healthy state, and to guide that voice to be in the healthiest communicating state, and to enable that student to gain enough knowledge of their voice and how it works that they can then make choices, and know what they're doing, and make decisions. Then there's the other side, which are people who are already established as performers living off those voices... we all get called by people who have been in the business for a long time and suddenly they've ticked a cross and they can no longer function. Or they're moving from mechanical media to having to do a live show and suddenly that voice won't do any more. Then maybe there is a way of the nodule, under supervision, going (if you like), being managed, even disappearing, as we've had with some actors – and yet the person being able to retain some of that quality of voice that's them in a healthy way. This happens a lot with singers, doesn't it? And with quite a lot of established actors – I know Judi Dench said she did reach a point where she'd lost it, and couldn't work, and then re-found it. It's walking a tightrope, there are no clear answers. But surely at the training stage I would say absolutely one needs to investigate, find out what's going on, teach ways of managing voice. Then it's up to that person what they do later in their career.

A: I don't think we should get too hung up on the idea of vocal nodules. Vocal disorders – unless there's an organic problem, there's been a long period of dysfunction that's led to a disorder. If I'm speaking to you like this [in a strained voice], I've got a slightly dysfunctional voice at this point. It might not be doing me any harm at all, but technically isn't this a bit of a dysfunctional voice that I'm now doing? But I may do this all of the time. So "dysfunction" means "a problem with function" in whose terms? In our terms as voice teachers, or in ordinary people's?

Z: The other thing we have to recognise is that, as we go through different stages in our life, our voice, vocal folds, the whole apparatus is changing, and sometimes there's a change that we don't understand. So the normal use that we've had is suddenly not working. That's not necessarily a dysfunction, it's literally a change. Certainly for women, there are huge menopausal changes. But also emotional – we can never disconnect the voice from the emotional, psychological, life-period crisis, whatever is happening.

Z: When you were talking with a strain in your voice, it's actually very hard to listen to it for any length of time. It makes me, personally, feel a pain in my own body in the same place. That, in reverse, is also the sort of healing property of theatre, when you can hear people using their voices in a way that reflects their whole emotional freedom, it then gives people the chance to be healed in that way themselves. Surely that's what we're all working towards.

H: My favourite singer for 30 years is Marianne Faithfull. I've watched her progress towards vocal disintegration. Her message is being communicated more and more strongly as her voice deteriorates – and that's not just me saying it, every review you'll read on any show or recording will say "What a wonderful excuse for cigarette smoking and for dissipated living". This is an artistic gem that has been finely honed through vocal ruination... . We've got to be so careful when we first meet the student. I've often met students whose first meeting with the voice teacher is a trauma. They feel for the first time, their voice – there's something wrong with them. It's a very bad beginning for them. So we have to be incredibly sensitive, I feel, and bear in mind there may be another Marianne Faithfull in the making...

A: It's a point about Maria Callas, who didn't have a disordered voice. But one of the things that was said about Callas was that part of her power was that vulnerability. You never quite knew if that voice was going to be reliable. And we humans want that – we warm to it, it connects to our hearts.

Z: People are more forgiving than perhaps we have convinced ourselves they ought to be. I think as voice practitioners we're almost looking for a reason, sometimes, to put people straight. I think members of the public and people in general – outside of the theatre I'm talking about now – are far more willing to accept these dysfunctional or irritating voices.

Z: They're not always irritating. My favourite singer is Tom Waits. I actually understand what you're saying, if you hear someone talk like that. But the voice you did, that kind of "creak", that's really popular in American movies. It's really appealing, people like it. I don't think a dysfunctional voice is always irritating. I don't think we do put up with it – we actually like it.

A: There's a big difference between the dysfunctional voice that can reach me, and the voice that doesn't reach me that is either not dysfunctional at all but there's a speech thing that somehow – there's a diction problem which means I can't comprehend, which is another issue – and a diction problem which I don't like because aesthetically it doesn't please me, which is another issue, but it's still not dysfunctional – but then the flat voice, the thing I don't find forgiving, because it switches me off.

Z: I think a voice can sound very attractive and very sexy in sharp bursts, which is fine in films. But what you were saying about losing the content – if that range is actually very limited, and they're delivering large chunks of text, then you can stop listening because you start hearing the fact that are actually only a few notes involved, and the pattern is very similar. I think that's quite important, particularly with teachers. There was some research done recently in Manchester hospitals – I don't know if you know about this, Christina – for 10-year-old primary school children. They had to watch three videos. There was one video by somebody with a voice within normal parameters, then there was somebody with a mildly dysfunctional voice and somebody with a severely dysfunctional voice, and they had to answer multiple-choice questions on these videos. Not surprisingly, the children scored better on the video where the passage was read by the person with the normal voice. But with the mildly dysfunctional voice and the severely dysfunctional voice, the results were almost the same, which was very interesting. So the children were not taking in the content, even from the mildly dysfunctional voice.

A: Yes, it said it didn't matter about the severity of the dysphonia, or the age or the gender of the child, or which school the child went to, because they tried it in different schools.

Z: Yes, they were across-the-board results.

A: There seems to be a feeling that we don't want some idealised voice. Because one thing implicit in what we're talking about is that if there is a dysfunctional voice, there is a fully functional voice, i.e., an ideal voice, which is of course what we're all not supposed to believe in. So we're agreed, as a group, that variation is a good thing and that variation may include what is sometimes called dysfunctional in terms of sound quality. Both

Marianne Faithfull and Tom Waits are singers, and singers are slightly different than speaking. I take the point myself that it depends how long it goes on, the voice. Don't let's forget the point that Ros made about the idea that the vibration in my voice goes into your body. That is a physical reality. Voice is a psychosomatic phenomenon. What comes from me has an effect on your body. So there are limits here.

Z: Can I just say something about the under-powered voice? I come across this quite a lot, every day when I answer the phone and I get somebody from a call centre, who is just going... I can't hear it. I have to say, "I'm sorry, I didn't get any of that, could you tell me again?" This seems to be happening quite a lot.

A: So would you define that as dysfunctional because it's not serving the purpose that it should be serving? The voice is not effective in that context? Is that a definition of dysfunction?

Z: It's one of mine, yes.

E: If nobody can understand what you're saying, if you're fundamentally not communicating, then I would say that was fairly dysfunctional. On stage we're drawing a distinction – somebody drew a distinction earlier between stage work and recorded work. It's very easy to go on with a dysfunctional voice if you're working in television or film. You can get away with it for a certain amount of time. But if you're doing a show from Monday to Saturday, twice on Tuesdays, twice on Saturdays, then that's going to show up after a while. If Tom Waits can do however many shows in a week and keep on, and keep that voice and not lose it, then his voice probably isn't dysfunctional. He's giving it support, he's caring for it, it's strong. He's connected, yes, absolutely.

Z: We can listen to anybody as long as they're really connected to what they're saying.

A: The question says: "Is the dysfunctional voice becoming commercial?" There's an implication there that 20 years ago it wouldn't have been around. What do people think?

Z: I'd agree with that. If you looked at television 20 years ago, programmes that were made in the 70s were still getting a little bit of "voice beautiful". If you look at television now, it's back to what somebody said about taking a natural voice. You were saying about BBC casting people actually actively now outsourcing their casting to go and find people. Films casting are looking for people off the street to star in films because they're the real thing, the raw talent.

Z: ...they want people because they happen geographically to have an address somewhere, to talk with the accent that they perceive comes from there. They live in London – they don't actually care whether the person has a real accent. You watch a programme that's supposed to be south west, and it's got the most awful cod accents.

E: There was a programme, Lovejoy, a few years ago, when you had West Country rhotic accents that you could hear, when it's supposed to be Suffolk! Suffolk is not a rhotic accent. It's an all-purpose, general country bumpkin kind of thing that they wanted.

Z: I think that's more insulting, really.

E: Yes, it is. But then the same distinction would not apply with something like Manchester or Birmingham or something like that because then they're very, very definite about it, and they know they're going to be accused of racism or regionalism or all sorts of things. But with this country bumpkin thing it doesn't apply – it's Suffolk and general West Country.

A: And is it some search for truth – some notion that "natural" equals "true"?

Z: I think that's right. Whether it's right or wrong, at bottom, I think that's what's going on. People are wanting – I think, having been an actor as well – to move away from a trained sound, as we were saying before. I worked with a guy who runs a voice-over agency, and I do some training with him. I said, "How about me doing some voice-over work?" and he said, "No, your voice is too nice." I said, "What do you mean?" He said, "You have no edge, no real accent, nothing people could really identify with." I was a bit shocked and upset – this is my voice! But I know what he means. I've worked quite hard to make a nice clear sound, and now I can't get a job doing voice-overs!

B: Is this the voice-quality thing in Spotlight? We now have to tick one box? Shouldn't they be able to do more? I'm telling them to tick them all. I'm sorry, I'm back to phonation, but they should be able to do harsh, husky, breathy, whatever. But that's commercially led, isn't it, by Spotlight?

Z: That's a very important point, this idea that you have to pigeonhole yourself. B was raising the question about the chameleon. Should we be aiming to train vocal chameleons? Are we not vocal chameleons?

B: I think we've always seen it as a parrot. That's how I present it to the students: that yes, you can do that very well, and you could go and work now with that sound, especially if they're talented. We get students arriving in the foundation unit and you think, wow, great, they could go and do that commercially, because they're so talented. But what we're trying to do is say: if you had to play a classical piece, could you do that? And of course they can't, they have a very limited range. And what we're saying is, yes; let's open the palette out so that you have choice.

Z: But reality TV supports the notion that in order to entertain... you don't need any training, you just need to be yourself.

Z: If you look at something like Big Brother, you talk about under-energising. It's amazing that it actually takes off because the lack of energy, and hours and hours of under-energised physicality and vocal energy that the British public is being exposed to on a regular basis is quite appalling.

Z: The dysfunctional voice is being commercially perpetrated to reflect an ever increasingly dysfunctional society, isn't it?

Z: I think the role of the ear is incredibly important. We were always exposed to a lot of oral – even then we weren't an oral culture, we've been a literate culture for a long time, but at least we had more live sound then. Nowadays I think people are generally exposed to electronic sound all the time – in which case often energy doesn't come into it, because that's all done by tweaking the buttons. So the physicality of breath and commitment to what we're saying is such a strong physical thing, we have to have the ears, if you like, to be able to cope with that. I think our hearing, our quality of hearing and our quality of intercourse, has been so dumbed down by the electronic media.

Z: I want to know what the ear perceives as sexiness in a husky voice, as opposed to somebody like, say, Brian Sewell, who has a very interesting voice, but it is very – well, I don't know – pardon me, I find it very non-sexy. I think that we've got two extremes there, but that's what society is at the moment: at the extreme. You've either got somebody who's got a unique voice like Sewell, and therefore he's entertaining because he's so extraordinary, or we've got somebody with a very husky, Mariella Frostrup sort of voice, who is in demand all the time.

H: When people talked about dysfunctional society, reality shows, television casting going out looking for people off the street – I think this is really the crux of the issue. This is where we're talking about the "given" voice versus the perceived "created" voice. We are at a time, I think, in our society where we do not – not just in voice work, but in any field – have much respect for the development of skill or the development of art, where it's a truly democratic society in its worse sense, I think, sometimes, where what's given – like what I've got is as good as what anybody else has got. So therefore don't tell me that even you need to work on this. So when you say in the question "Is it becoming more popular?" – yes, it is becoming more popular and the given voices often can be dysfunctional. In fact the dysfunctionality is a sign that it truly is a given voice and not a worked-on voice, and I think that's a crux of this whole issue. And it's such a large issue, and it's very interesting that we, from our little corner, are working on it, but it's such a gigantic issue – it's so much bigger than what we're doing today. We're just talking about one small outward vocal sign of a gigantic movement in our society today.

A: It's to do with my interest always in the psychosomatic aspects of voice. If I start to talk like this *[her voice drops]*, this is going to have an effect on your body. Which is why I can't agree that teachers' voices don't matter. When my son is trapped with one teacher all day long, and they're talking like this, it's having an effect on him, I believe. The sexy voice is produced generally by swollen vocal folds, yes? And there is more air escape than normal. My hypothesis is that if you have swollen vocal folds, there is a suggestion that other folds of your body might well be swollen as well, all right? We have to talk frankly here. And that the vocal cords are open – there is more breath coming through – so other parts of your body may also be open. Now that is just a hypothesis, you can take it or leave it. But I think there is a fascinating speculative thing here, which is that if you look at – and I'm talking here only about women's voices, male voices are also interesting – but if you look at the inside of the larynx or the inside of the... the top of the vagina... this is all being recorded, but it's absolutely true! When my husband first saw *[inaudible]* stroboscopy, he said: "Goodness! What part of the body is that?" There is a fascinating thing that Jenogra Williams, who is one of the specialists on the adolescent voice, told me, that when you look histologically at a scraping from the cervix and a scraping from the vocal folds, the cells are very, very similar. So it's not just entirely fantasy here, but it is something about... there are other things like the sexy voice often suggests this open tract which suggests a relaxation, and you have to be fairly relaxed to have sex. Well, we're generalising here, but, you know: "You're going to have a better time with me if I'm relaxed than if I'm uptight." So there are all sorts of physiological, psychosomatic reasons why the sexy voice taps into us. I say to my students, if you're saying: *[in a strained voice]* "Would you like to have a cup of coffee with me?" you're not going to be as successful as if you say *[in a relaxed voice]* "Would you like to come and have a cup of coffee with me?" Really. There are physical reasons, but we've lost that kind of grit connection to the body of voice, which is why working with the Roy Hart Theatre is so utterly wonderful, and certainly has transformed my life. But that's enough on that.

[they break and answer the topic question privately...then present their conclusions]

J: "A voice which is constricted or damaged in such a way as to impede effective communication."

Z: "A voice which is produced in such a way to cause damage to the vocal cords, often difficult to listen to; a voice which is unconnected to the real centre of the human being in a degree to dysfunction in relating to others, and it's a spectrum along which we're all travelling to complete freedom."

Z: "A voice that sounds painful, either because it's husky or it's creaking or the vocal signal is interrupted in some way so that it's difficult to listen to. You're more aware of the sound than you are of the message."

Z: "Physical malfunction causing vocal harm." Or: "A missing aspect of vocal production that impedes communication or understanding, i.e., volume, articulation, emotional *[inaudible]* connection."

Z: "Dysfunctional voice is a voice that is unable to function properly for the task in hand, and therefore blocks communication."

E: "The inability to communicate effectively, personally or professionally."

Z: "A voice which from speaker and/or listener's view does not achieve the desired result within the given context."

Z: "A voice which does not fulfil the function of communication."

Z: "Inasmuch as the voice is a function of the need to express, communicate and reinforce an individual's place in a group or society, it is also a way in which the collective communicates its existential dilemma. Anything that fails to do this is dysfunctional."

A: "Dysfunctional voice has two meanings: a voice which, in its quality, suggests an unhealthy function of muscle and tissue which may or may not lead to vocal fold damage; or, a voice which is different in one or more parameters from what we as voice practitioners feel is a free and healthy sound. There is an infinite variety of voice qualities to be heard in ordinary voices. What matters is that the voice (a) reflects the truth of the person; (b) works for the context, singing or spoken; (c) does no damage to voicer or to listener."

Z: "A voice that is unable to create an authentic, congruent and expressive bridge between the inner experience of the speaker – mental, emotional and psychological – with the inner world of the listener."

Z: "A dysfunctional voice is one that's unclear, one that has to be repeated in order to transmit some sort of communication; also, one that's inarticulate – part of the same thing – and under-powered: one that has to be increased in volume so that the hearer can obviously pick up what they're trying to say; and also, a voice that's tight."

H: "A dysfunctional voice is a voice which is not sustainable without causing physical damage, or a voice which does not serve the speaker or the listener in the communication of the message at all levels – physical, emotional or intellectual."

Z: Something inside of me feels that dysfunctional voice – and I might be completely on a different planet here – is something more to do with phonation level, whereas for me vocal dysfunction leads more into the connection with the message and the communication.

Z: I think we have to be a little bit careful about judging what we hear. Obviously our society – we're obviously in this space, in this journey towards freedom and we have to acknowledge that, yes, a voice might break down, and we might be subjected through television and radio, through performance, to voices that people will listen to and say: "Well, I don't like to listen to that, that constant noise, that voice makes me feel uncomfortable." Sometimes, you know, we have to feel uncomfortable.

Z: The question originally, which one of us summed up so beautifully, was "Is the dysfunctional voice becoming more commercial?" It's only us that are calling it dysfunctional, as you say. In the outside world most people wouldn't think that's a dysfunctional voice. So the media are, as always, actually following society in this. So we have to be careful. We're sitting in judgement on something... in fact, what we're really doing, in a sense, is trying to make sense of what we do as trainers.

A: So what are the implications for training, then?

H: I feel that we have agreed very much with B: we have the voices we deserve as a society, we have the voices we want as a society. And at the moment we're very uncertain. We're big on personal choices that are baffling us, etc., and we're a little bewildered, and our voices reflect that. On the other hand, I feel that, as voice teachers, we have – and this is what struck me listening to Ros earlier – her vision. We must have some vision. What are we going to give? Not just "we're going to help somebody to speak better". But what is it that we stand for? What I feel I stand for, as a voice teacher, is more power, more clarity, more confidence as a speaker. So that's what we can bring in our little way to this bewildered society speaking in its bewildered voices. Clarity, confidence, power, many other things too – these are just examples. Because we have to say, yes, we must recognise where we're at as a society and how we fit into that, but we also have to realise: what do we bring to this society? We recognise where the society is, and therefore the sort of voices it speaks with and appreciates, but how can we do our little? So it's a balance. We must recognise where the society is, where we are in the society, but then ask ourselves: what is our vision? We're not just another reality show.

Z: ...could it not be that a functional voice would be even more commercial were it on offer, and were people enabled with it, and were listeners offered the treat of it?

H: I just feel that, to answer that quickly, I think that maybe the voice we're offering is not the most commercial, and I don't think it will be, and I don't think we can make it so. Because in truth it doesn't reflect the society as it is today. So we have to sell an uncommercial product, or we have to give up our vision and offer ways of speaking like Mariella Frostrup.

Z: I would really dispute that, though, because given the choice, most people – and we'll leave the husky quality out of it – but most people respond more to a wide-ranging and native voice they can hear, they can feel connected emotionally in someone. So it may be not less as commercially viable, but simply on offer as much. You're talking like actors have stopped letting us understand, but people would mostly like to hear what they say.

Z: ...I think if I had to choose one word, I'd choose "flexibility", because for me my own voice exploration has taken me into places and states of being and emotional exploration that I would never have gone into otherwise, and that in the Roy Hart work, for instance, where you let your voice go into these places it would never go. Little bits of that are then available to you. So "chameleon" implies for me a kind of falsity. But actually we do adapt. My voice is different now, because I'm going to go home at the end of a very long day – I started at four this morning – and talk to my husband, I'm not going to have this [voice], I'm going to do something else. If, on the other hand, I had to do something extraordinary, I could do it, and that's what I think has to happen. It links also to the whole concept of the word "commercial". I totally take the point about society, and if we take the sitcoms, they are reflecting so much of society. But we also have Bleak House, we also have Shakespeare. We also have voice-overs. We have a huge variety of things where voices are for sell, and I think our job is to ensure that people can do any of that, and that they don't lose their natural voice.

B: ..."commercial" means distinctive, and in order to be distinctive, you need all those little armourings, all those little protective things that people do. You know, the lisp – Frank Muir – the stammer, all of these things... that's what I mean about – what we have to steer clear of, I think, is: "I'm a voice teacher, I have to teach optimal vocal function." I think that becomes then a problem. If we are saying, "Yes, you have to open up the individual so that they can go places that are very extreme" – absolutely. Because you have to be able to do extremely excruciating noises, unsocial noises, but do them safely, because then that reflects society. But I think we're getting a bit of a problem between the message and the speech. They're the way in which the medium is sculpted and becomes the message. That's the message, and Brian Sewell is giving the message. I mean he gets his message across. People are going to switch off if they don't like his voice quality, but those are two very different things.

Z: The people that you mentioned as possibly having dysfunction are all great communicators.

B: Absolutely.

Z: So they're not really dysfunctional.

B: That's why I would say maybe we have to separate this between the dysfunction and the commercial. Maybe we use a term like: we're teaching commercial voice? Or the idiosyncratic voice? It's all about flexibility.

Z: Exactly.

Z: I think the term "vocal distinction" is a very interesting word, because often the commercial voice has a distinction. A lot of us were trained as voice teachers to believe that actually the best thing about the voice is that the audience doesn't notice it, because it serves the text and the character, and actually the commercial voice often does have a peccadillo that is memorable and gets attached to that person. Then again we're into the cult of personality and celebrity, which is exactly what we've been talking about.

Z: For everybody, their whole body is their instrument, their voice is their instrument, so what you really want to make available for people is the range of their instrument, to use it safely and to give them the widest possibility of choices so that they can then decide what they do themselves.

A: Do we not agree with that as being the implication for training, what you've just said?

All: Yes.

Z: ...the image that keeps coming back in our final bits of discussion, in opening up that flexibility (if you want to call it that), or teaching healthy vocal function and being able to produce so many different sounds, is the tool box. I don't know, we might... it's just an image for me. You can pick up anything out of that tool box, and the idea is to fill that tool box up with all these different options, but at the base of it is the box, and that's your healthy vocal function and awareness of your voice through the years of working, and to support it all, each voice being unique to that speaker. That's what you were saying: that you're freest within you.

H: I think it's one thing we can take from what we were saying about the dysfunctional society and the dysfunctional voice. Society today tends to go for the given voice. That's a gift to us, really, because for a long time we didn't truly believe in the given voice. We felt that that was just raw material out of which to make something perfect. And if we can learn anything today from the situation in which we find ourselves, it's that the given voice is the place to start. And the given voice in itself, the voice that we're starting with – we may help it to work better, we may help it to cause less damage to itself, but in fact it is the beginning and the end of the work in some way. So that's something to take away from our problem in trying to define this.

A: I'd like to thank you all, and I hope you, like me, have found it a most stimulating discussion.

Chapter 11
Plenary – Summation by Chairs of the Discussions of the Day

CAROL FAIRLAMB: I was in the "Voice in the Conservatoire" session. It wasn't altogether positive... [Laughter] It's against my nature, really, to have to deliver bad news. A lot of people in the session felt that it's a very difficult time to be a voice teacher in a conservatoire setting, not least because there is some confusion about what a conservatoire actually is. There was a lot of confusion about that, mainly because of the fact that a lot of courses now have university status but are also conservatoires. There is a mixing of academia and practical training. So that confusion led to some difficulty in terms of our roles. Related to that, some distrust I've got of academia in terms of teaching practical skills, a distrust of research and the sort of research that we're being asked to do in these settings. Not necessarily my own view, but I'm passing on what was said.

There is strong concern about the standard of students that are coming through onto courses, and how best we can serve them. Are we serving them well? Not in what we're offering in class – that was very positive – but in the wider world, whether when they leave are they at all likely to get work? And should we be responsible for that? Most people felt incredibly responsible for that aspect of things. What happens to them when they go? Although, interestingly, one of the MAVS students put forward the view that, actually, should we be responsible for that? Other degree courses don't say that if you train as a building surveyor, you're necessarily going to get work as a building surveyor. So should we take that responsibility on, or not? But the general view was that we do, and we worry about the moral and ethical implications, and that feeds very deeply into our work and what Ros was saying earlier about us as people, not just in our role as voice teachers.

On the positive side, I asked people if they could see the next hundred years. We tend to look back on the last hundred years with admiration and respect for what's gone before – I think I'm speaking for everybody here when I say that – but in the next hundred years how would we want people meeting in this theatre now to be seeing us then? The general feeling was perhaps that they would see us as people who kept on going [Laughter] in spite of it all – kept working to standards and kept working in the way that we feel is right.

JOE WINDLEY: I was doing the "Voice in Higher Education" session. One of the things that did emerge throughout the day was that there was a strong sense that we don't have a strong, common voice. That came up this morning, and it came up this afternoon, and I think that there is something there, for all of us to consider: what do we want? And the other – and this is just a taster, this worked its way right through the process – what is voice learning? And how does it impact upon the HE sector? Not just in terms of the student experience, but also how does it impact upon teaching styles? What kind of models are represented within the subject and other subjects within HE? From that it began to – this afternoon particularly – snowball out into: Where is voice taught as part of a life-affirming experience? So we were looking at it not only in actor training contexts, but also in terms of the subject itself and how it celebrates the human condition, or potentially suppresses the human condition? So it seems that there are a lot of questions that need to be asked there.

There was also a discussion about; what is a voice module? If you've had a two-hour hit, does that mean that you've had voice training? So what is the word "training", what is the word "education", and what is the word "learning", and how do they impact on the subject and the environment within which the subject is being addressed? And a very clear sense that – and this picks up from what Ros was saying this morning – it's the people that regulate that actually often need the educating. There is the will coming from younger people, the interest and the capacity and the talent, but somehow voice in the UK does not seem to be at the heart of what the learning process or what the educational process is, from those who seem to be controlling policy, ironically happening under a government that is talking a lot about inclusion. So it's not just actually the inclusion, it's actually what do you follow through with? How do you let the inclusion inform the overall environment within which the learning is occurring?

JOHN WILD: Ours was "Voice in the Community", so I'll talk about the first group. The key points that we looked at were language and education, health aspects of the voice work, and problems of overcoming difficulties. We had a room full of experts, and it was really difficult to stay silent – that doesn't mean myself – and really listen for an hour and a half. It's really interesting because one of the main points that came out of that was "learning to listen within the community". What are we listening for within a community? Are we listening to speech or voice? We looked at language, and talked about: are we really looking at the clarity of articulation, or the sense behind the words? Is it the way we speak, or what we speak? That comes from her experience. And the Englishness in English: are we looking at American English? Asian? Black? We're dealing with lots of many Englishes. So the solution to that is that we have to hijack the educational establishment and go right back to the roots of where language is first explored, where sounds are first explored. How do we do that? Again, that could be an ongoing debate, and we could have talked about it for the rest of the day, but we didn't.

So there is a distinction and a conflict between voice and speech. So we started to look at: are we dealing with voice and vocal therapy, or speech, language, articulation, elocution, and so on and so forth? And when we look at their voices, when we're working on speech, are we looking at standard English – which still frightens a lot of people – people were saying, when we look at standard English, do we frighten them away from looking at their voices? Because there is still this element of: are we working the shaping of sound, or sound? Then we talked about voice and the individual: voice being therapy, helping with illness; voice being an identity, helping us understand who we are; voice being sound that resonates between cultural divides. Is there some misunderstanding of what we are dealing with, if we think about that more deeply? Are we connecting with who we are through our sound, or are we creating sound to convince others of who we are?

So I was working to summarise the first group. Are we all searching outside ourselves in the community to understand voice in the community, or should we be looking within ourselves, within our community, which is our voice? Then there was a wonderful conclusion. One of the participants said: "The word 'the voice' is very difficult to digest." So the rest of the group debated that, and maybe there should be a different verb. Maybe we should be using "voicing". I know Barbara Houseman used the words "sound shaping", which is quite interesting. At the end I asked everybody else to summarise, and they came up with the words: "vocal help", "my voice", "misunderstanding", "listening", "sense and clarity". So I'd summarise by: "vocal community within ourselves, meeting the vocal community without".

During this afternoon's group, we touched upon cultural conflict, because it relates to what the group was talking about this morning. Communication of our work within the community: I think that's something we have to think about. "Vocal immigration" was another topic we looked at this afternoon, and that was a delicate subject to approach. We're crossing cultural divides. There was a lot of cultural mix within the group, and I think we dealt with that very well. And learning to listen to those cultural divides: through them, at them… Does that mean our listening attitudes have to change in the work? So there is a delicate balance. On a positive side: it's a very exciting time for voice work, being in a cultural situation. The simple choices that we can offer can make so much difference to the voices in community. We talked about the breath: the simplicity of breathing and standing in space. The people outside the drama school establishments and technical establishments: those simple things mean so much to these people, and underlining that was quite a passionate connection and understanding that for us, it was quite difficult – I think it still is – to understand that when we listen and hear people. Again, finishing on a high note: realising that everyone has ribs and a diaphragm!

CLAUDETTE WILLIAMS: We talked about **"The Urban Voice"**, and what is it? We talked about it as an intercultural mix that is the voice of youth, and how as voice teachers can we use that within our work? How can we make voice relate to young people? So… yow! [Laughter]

ALEX BINGLEY: And we looked at it, not only in terms of dialect, but also in terms of: how do we incorporate the urban voice into the totality of training? So that, for instance, we are not working on vowels and resonance within a standard English/RP model. So certainly we have to look into the urban voice more specifically in terms of its intonation, its rhythm… in terms of breaking it down phonetically. Also we felt that, within a drama school environment, is creating an environment wherein the student may discover their own cultural identity. Yes, the urban voice is important, but also they need to move from that, they need to move from their sense of themselves into something else, be it standard English, be it Glaswegian, be it Welsh, whatever. Something positive to ring false to them is that this is something that this cultural group has found in an age of internet technology and jargon and sound bite, when all of us are going: "but the word is being destroyed"… Here is something that has been created by the youth of today, and once they have found that they can discover that, they have done that, there is then not quite such a big leap from that to, say, Shakespeare or to Webster or whatever. Perhaps another way of getting them to discover this urban voice, to discover the sense of their own identity, is to teach *us* an accent: something not within that they have been taught. So within sort of standard English, Glasgow, Dublin accent, but something completely different. Jamaican, for instance. That they can teach us, using the phonetic skills that they have been given earlier in the term.

CLAUDETTE: We also looked at the urban voice as far as: within your school, is there one black student in a year group? How does that student cope? I've had stories from teachers who have said that a student has taken them aside and said: "I cannot actually cope, because I feel depth of fear." So how do we empower students of differing backgrounds? Within my teaching it comes from the spoken word. I use a wide variety of poetry, usually African-American. What are we doing to bring about changes within the modules? Is there cross-cultural work going on? So that the students are leaving speaking from RP to an urban sound, affording a level of choice. I feel incredibly privileged to stand in two worlds: my love of Shakespeare, and an incredibly vibrant culture. And I wish you to share that.

KATERINA MORAITIS: So I'm going to start off with summing up what happened in the **"Ring Tone vs Vocal Tone"** group; we had a smaller group than most, so we had a little more of an intimate relationship with what we were all saying, it was lovely. The first thing we came up with was that technology, if you like, is going in one direction, and it's going so quickly and so fast that we as people – not only as voice coaches but also as teachers – find it difficult to keep up. I know the older we get as well, the more difficult it is to deal with the terminology and the way that we deal with particular computer-generated models of all sorts of things.

So it was felt very strongly at first that technology was the enemy, and that technology was something that was taking us away from the way that we want to use voice, which is feeling the resonance of the voice, understanding the communications between two human beings rather than a human being and a machine. It was then evident straightaway, however – someone said that it was wonderful to hear a friend of hers over the internet, and hear her voice coming through, and there was a sense of that communication, and being able to touch somebody else's soul, and touch somebody else physically, even though it was over an electronic medium. There's a lot of work done with technology: the blue screen, working with actors who have to work with characters who aren't there, characters who have to be a monster, characters who have to be holding themselves up a castle, as in the example of Harry Potter's new film.

We decided that we wanted a marriage of the two. We wanted the good things of that technology, we wanted to work *with* technology, so that there was a marriage going on, the two of them working together in harmony. How lovely is that? However, we also felt that there was... technology bred a mistrust. That there is a superficiality that happened with technology. Things can be air-brushed, voices can be enhanced. You may no longer need to be a pop singer: you can just have the look, be recorded, and somebody will technologically enhance your voice so that it sounds more resonant or it's more articulate, and sound in a particular way. What we didn't want, however, was that superficiality and that recording of the voice that we feel is also going into theatre nowadays. So that even on a very small level, when you go to the opera or musical theatre, you're actually hearing voices that are coming from microphones rather than coming through the natural resonance of the voice. We don't want, however, to throw the baby out with the bath water. What we decided we wanted were voices that were more grounded, not less grounded, but steeped more in training and in the work that we are doing on breath support, in terms of intelligibility – that actually technology means that that is needed more, not less. We wanted to educate directors; we want to educate those people who use technology, we want to educate computer technicians, we want educate people who are using voice-enhancing systems, and possibly we want to embrace the internet in a verbal way and in an oral way, rather than just a written way. So having discussion groups where you can actually use a microphone and have discussions with other people across the seas, which I thought was a brilliant idea. In other words we said we wanted patience, and working in harmony with technology.

CHRISTINA SHEWELL: We had: **"Is the Dysfunctional Voice Becoming Commercial?"** One of the great strengths was, we had two large groups, and – as I'm sure everybody found, whether the group was big or small, a wonderful mix of people – and that is extremely rich and I think a great credit to this whole day. I'm not going to try and summarise those groups separately, but these seemed to be welcome additions, the main issues: the first was this big discussion about "What is dysfunctional voice?"

I actually ended up asking everybody to write down a definition and then read it. So that will be on the tape, and at some point I guess we'll be able to read all these definitions. It feels like they fell into three groups. One is to do with health: you know, the unhealthy voice, and how important it is for us as voice teachers to really know that we may need to refer on. However, some people can manage with amazing pathologies, either in terms of structure or in terms of how they use, and we can't be too prescriptive here. The second aspect of dysfunctional voice was the whole concept of the emotional connection, that actually you may say "What a sweet, high voice I have", but actually if it doesn't feel right to me, or conversely it feels right to me and not to you, then there is an emotionally dysfunctional voice. But that does connect to the third one, which is the listener judgement, which opened up the hugely interesting area: we're always so careful, aren't we, to say we don't believe in one good and true voice. But actually the concept of dysfunctional voice implies that somewhere we believe there is a functional voice.

However, we discussed this and talked about it, and then we talked about what generally is meant by the dysfunctional voice – the husky voice, the sexy voice, the constricted, energetic voice, the loud voice, and how we hear this all the time on adverts, voice-overs, sitcoms and so on.

We also touched on singing, about which, I think we would all agree, there is much more to say. And that singers like Marianne Faithfull, Tom Waits, Rod Stewart, make a living from their "dysfunctional sound", which we wouldn't call dysfunctional on one level. We agreed that actors can do all sorts of dysfunctional vocal behaviours. We ended up, at the end of the second group, almost throwing out the word "dysfunctional". It's of very limited use. We can talk about aspects of the voice that don't help, but to condemn a voice as dysfunctional, I think we're onto slightly rocky ground there. Actors can do all sorts of things at different times, but they do need technique to underpin, if they're going to do them a lot.

An interesting point came up that society is dysfunctional itself and likes dysfunctional voices. *[Laughter]* We want real voices, real edgy people in the Big Brother room. We don't want them to sound like trained actors. And that there is a distrust now – if we think back to the Olivier days – we don't want a voice like that, we don't trust it any more. (That's not meant to be an imitation of Olivier!) You know the kind of voice. So we want "real people", whatever that means. That was a most interesting area of discussion.

But the conclusion, and the last remark this afternoon, was that if we have a connected, full voice with enough training, most actors and speakers can take a few "disses".

JOE: Obviously we're building upon the wonderful work that was done through the ICV that David Carey started. There is a legacy, but then the future happens, and let's keep that sense going. The other thing is that the ICV is for us. It's not international on its own. Certainly if we get a lot of people from London, it'll have an international element, but it is for us. What do you want from today? What do you want, where do you want to go? How do we interface with society? We raised so many questions, it would be awful if we fell into the trap of: "We discussed that, and then some time passed, and nothing happened". We can help. We can provide the facility. The thing that's more important than budget – and there is something that's more important than budget – is the human spirit, and the human spirit of a voice teacher proactive in the subject is wonderful. So I appeal to you to be rigorous about your expectations about the ICV. Come and join in. Be energetic. Let's get something going, and let's keep this conduit for exchange going, because we owe it to the subject and we owe it to the people that we work with, and strength in numbers, and so on…

Appendix 1: Feedback Sheet
The Contemporary Voice
How We Teach Voice in the New Millennium

7th January 2006 – Feedback Sheet

Please rate the following areas (1 being highest, 5 lowest)

Networking Possibilities	1	2	3	4	5
Usefulness of Discussion					
Session 1 (state)	1	2	3	4	5
Session 2 (state)	1	2	3	4	5
Keynote Speaker (am)	1	2	3	4	5
Afternoon Introduction	1	2	3	4	5

What did you enjoy most about the day?

_____

_____

What would you like to see included/developed if we were to do a similar event next year?

_____

_____

If we were not able to subsidise the event next year, how much would you be prepared to pay to attend?

☐ Under £25   ☐ £25 - £50   ☐ £50-£75   ☐ £75+

Any other comments:

_____

_____

_____

_____

Thank you for taking the time to fill in this survey.
Please return it at the end of the day to the desk in the foyer.

Appendix 2: Feedback Returns for ICV Event 7th Jan - Graphs

Ratings (1 highest, 5 lowest)

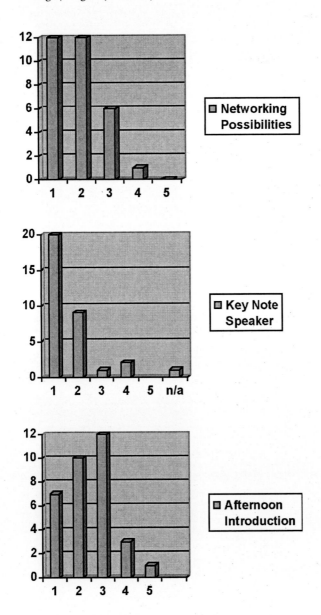

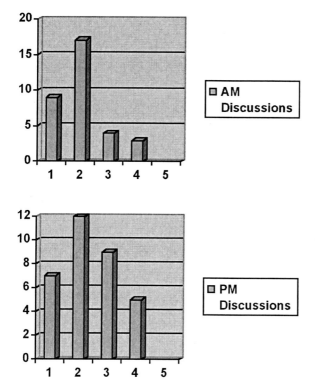

Appendix 3: Feedback Returns for ICV Event 7th Jan – Comments

1. What did you enjoy most about the day?

Listening and debating

The opportunity to talk to other voice teachers

Sitting all together in the theatre

Opportunity to exchange ideas with other practitioners

Hearing many points of view and exchanging ideas

A sense of community with similar interests and concerns

The vast pool of ideas and experience of each person and the openness of mind to go into the future

As one can only do 2 groups, I really enjoyed the 3.30 summing up. I loved listening to Ros' and Joes' questions – very stimulating

Seeing colleagues

Meeting other practitioners

Exchange of opinions

Opportunity to meet and talk with colleagues and new acquaintances

Listening/Being a Chair

A gathering of voice teachers. New information. Stimulating ideas. A broad, cross section of practise represented

Talking with peers

Discussion of crucial themes and problems

Meeting other voice teachers and discussing passionately things which are current in the vocal world

Opportunity to meet, to talk, to discuss

Professional exchange – increased awareness of what other people are talking about

An opportunity to talk about voice with other tutors where discussions openly was the point

Being with others in the profession, networking, listening and sharing

The discussion: Ring tone or vocal tone

The mix of people and experiences – the open opportunity given to speak in non-judgemental environment

Meeting old friends. Re thinking a bit – good for me

Morning key-note speech

Starting a dialogue with voice colleagues

Meeting different practioners

Meeting other practitioners – hearing their points of view – having time to sit back, listen and talk about voice and being a voice teacher – and what that means personally and in a wider context

The opportunity to connect with other voice teachers

The opportunity to meet friends and colleagues in discussion about common issues

2. What would you like to see included/developed if we were to do a similar event next year?

Looking at where do we go with voice in the 21st century

Questions after Ros's talk

More of the same – perhaps something experimental

Perhaps practical classroom/hands on. Suggestions for us on how to realise the discussed aims

Discussions and maybe a group sounding beginning at end of the day. Concessions for over 65s (price wise)

Voice in the business community; voice in self-expression

The follow-up for the Voice in HE and Conservatoire groups; and move on working in an industry that has a lot of technology

One hour long round tables

Perhaps expand to a 2 day event

Possibility of people having 5/10 minutes to share findings/research/networking with a captive audience

More focus on work in action to achieve aims

Coffee ! chatting over breaks is good!

"Solidarity" of voice teachers in getting their work recognised in HE

More mixed debate

Another good speaker? Lecture on an aspect of voice – illustrated, more networking

More time for discussion as didn't quite get to the core

More time for group response at the end

Interactive workshops – would like to experience Roy Hart

Challenging keynote addresses – possibly including question and answer on the address

A wider spectrum of voice practitioners. Open the house to questions to the keynote speaker

Bring some directors in?

Smaller groups for the discussions

Perhaps a tighter focus on a smaller range of issues

More breaks, water for all. Longer lunch (1 ½ hours)

3. Any other comments

Excellent Day

We need to build the links between the freelancers and those working in institutions

Thank you x 7

So much commitment, loves, passion for voice, language and expertise – in the world of artistic endeavour, drama, theatre and the musical world

A need for a 'voice' that takes voice into education more freely – a voice doesn't tick boxes

I found the day very stimulating but I could have coped with longer – I know there's logistics and travelling, etc. and location, but 2 of these a year or more maybe – so our collective consciousness slowly seeps into the community and towards the powers that make the decisions, that our collective voice is truly heard, so Hoe's next film will show the results of the voice teachers' influence

Re paying: nothing – at a push £25 or under

We need to make sure the chair is clearer about the questions

Re paying - £50 for two days

Coffee on arrival – but that was excused!

Thanks for setting it up

Really nice day

A great idea – really hope ICV can get off the ground and become a professional body with an identity and eventually some influence. I think developing education, discussion and rehearsals will help this process

A really good day – one a year would be good

Would love to see this developed as a conference for voice

If possible, please keep going – a great day – wasn't too sure this morning when woke up (!) but really enjoyed the day – thank you

Chair should clarify questions/statements and structure the sessions to avoid anecdotal chat (comment based on various discussions)

Very good day – well done everybody!

Enjoyable day – hope it grows teeth in making our voices heard in the larger community

Appendix 4: Chair Biographies

Carol Fairlamb is a freelance voice and dialect coach having been awarded a Post-graduate Diploma in Voice Studies in 1995. She has taught voice for several drama schools including: Central, Rose Bruford, Drama Centre, Oxford School of Drama, Italia Conti and the Academy of Live and Recorded Arts. She also coaches corporate clients. Carol Fairlamb is currently researching how theatre directors can make best use of voice coaches in the rehearsal room.

Katerina Moraitis is a Lecturer in Voice at Central School of Speech and Drama. She gained her Postgraduate qualification in Voice from Central School of Speech and Drama in 1997/98. She is the only Certified Lessac Specialist in the United Kingdom. Katerina Moraitis was Head of Voice at Northumbria University from 1998 to 2004 and in that time worked with leading North-East theatre companies, such as Northern Stage and Live Theatre. Katerina has studied, coached and taught voice internationally at the Actors Studio, National Institute of Dramatic Art and New York University. She is currently North-East Associate Editor for the International Dialects of English Archive. She is currently working on investigation into sensory approaches to performance.

John Wild is an actor, director, and Head of Voice at ALRA. He has recently been asked to join the board of the ICV.

Claudette Williams is a Lecturer of Voice at Central School of Speech and Drama. She gained her postgraduate diploma in Voice at Central School of Speech and Drama. Since 2001, she has worked as Voice consultant for the Royal National Theatre *Elmina's Kitchen* winner of Evening Standard Award; the Royal Court/Tawala Theatre Co. Productions, *Blest Be The Tie* by Dona Daley; Tricycle Theatre/Tawala Theatre Co. Productions *Blues for Mr. Charlie*; Nottingham Playhouse Mother Courage Emma – Award Nomination. Claudette Williams has written plays for Radio 4, and several reviews for *Spare Ribs* magazine. Claudette Williams is an acting member of the Royal Shakespeare Company.

Joe Windley is the Course Leader and Principle Lecturer on the MA Voice Studies at Central School of Speech and Drama.

Bruce Wooding is Head of the School of Professional and Community Development at the Central School of Speech and Drama. He was previously Head of Drama at an Inner London Comprehensive School and a lecturer in Drama Education since 1996. He has also worked as an external examiner for Chester College. In 2003 he was appointed as Head of Professional Development and Lifelong Learning. His research work includes work for Westminster Schools (1993); contribution to Ch.7 *Making Media; practical production media education,* Buckingham et al. (1994); work for Harbinger School (1996); and a research project in Ghana - investigating Arts provision (1997-8), researching effectiveness at Lyric Theatre, Hammersmith (1999-2000); research for the London Borough of Newham looking into Arts & Learning Styles (2001); and he completed research – Playwriting with *Young Offenders* (2002). In 2003 he was featured in 'The Guardian' 'Theatre Idol' article where Bruce worked with a rapper and a boy band member developing audition skills. He undertook consultancy work for Walt Disney International. In 2004 he worked with

Endemol TV company presenting a show called *Misunderstood*. He completed a chapter for a CADISE wide research project into disability and the arts. He was part of a research team for Arts Aimhigher who visited Miami to investigate the notion and practice of *Portfolio Day* (2005).

Bruce Wooding has presented work at the IDEA conference, Kenya: 'The/A Black Voice in English Drama Education'; at the NATD conference - working with Dorothy Heathcote and also explored educational drama and intercultural influences in Ghana.

His written work includes *Multicultural Education - a consideration of perspectives* for the Theatre Centre and *Authoring Identity* in 'Drama 11-18' ed. Nicholson H, 2000.

Appendix 5: ICV Information

The International Centre for Voice was established in October 2000 in order to serve the professional development of teachers of voice and speech.

The principal aims of the Centre are:

- to create and maintain a professional forum, resource base and network for voice teachers and other interested professionals
- to provide training and professional updating for voice teachers
- to promote research and development in the field of vocal pedagogy.

At the beginning of the 21st century, The Central School of Speech and Drama launched The International Centre for Voice, based at the School, to serve the professional development of teachers of voice and speech.

The International Centre for Voice has three main aims:

1 To create and maintain a professional forum, resource base and network for voice teachers and other interested professionals by establishing:

- formal links with allied professional organisations
- an international directory for voice teachers
- a website and internet discussion group.

2 To provide training and professional updating for voice teachers by offering:

- refresher courses and further specialist training for established teachers of voice and speech
- an advice and consultancy service for voice teachers working across the spectrum of voice teaching
- voice and dialect coaching in the professional theatre, film and television, voice and speech in actor training, voice and song, voice and movement, voice and speech with professional voice users, and voice and speech for personal development.

3 To promote research and development in the field of voice teaching by establishing:

- a journal for the documentation and dissemination of good practice across the spectrum of voice teaching.

Advisory Board

Cicely Berry - Voice Director for the Royal Shakespeare Company
David Carey - RADA
Geoffrey Colman - Head of Acting, Central School of Speech and Drama
Mr D. Garfield Davies - Consultant Laryngologist
Carol Fairlamb - Freelance voice coach
Joan Mills - Head of Voice, Centre for Performance Research
Jean Moore - Head of Voice, School of Drama (RSAMD)
Antony Tuckey - Former Artistic Director of the Wolsey Theatre, Ipswich
John Wild - Head of Voice (ALRA)
Bruce Wooding - Head of the School of Professional and Community Development,
Central School of Speech and Drama

Archives

The ICV hosts an archive of relevant and interesting archive materials relating to voice and speech. We are hoping to create a resource that can be used by all interested voice professionals aiding research and development within the field of voice teaching. The materials have, to date, been donated and include signed copies of books and manuscripts.

We have received many donations from around the world and are in the process of developing a scheme whereby those that have bequeathed entire libraries of resource to us will be awarded lifetime membership of the ICV in recognition of their generosity. We are also in the process of looking at ways of generating materials for the archive. If you have written a book or paper for a conference which you feel you would like to donate as part of the archive then please do not hesitate to contact the Centre. All items donated to the archive are clearly labelled to recognise the individual who donated the item. The Centre also welcomes suggestions as to material that we should be looking to acquire.

International Centre for Voice Membership

Full Individual Membership*

Open to fully qualified or practising teachers of voice and speech along with any qualified professional from any allied organisation offering close links to the teaching of voice and speech.

Full individual members are entitled to:
• 2 Newsletters by post and/or e-mail
• Advance notification of forthcoming ICV events along with priority booking
• Notification of forthcoming national and international events
• Full access to Central School of Speech and Drama library inclusive of external loan rights, inclusive of access to ICV archive materials
• All applications for Full membership must be accompanied by an up-to-date CV.

Full Institutional Membership

This membership entitles three institutional colleagues to join simultaneously with one membership card.

Student Membership

Open to any student training to teach voice and speech. Open to all who have an interest in voice and speech.

Student Members are entitled to:
• 2 Newsletters by post and/or e-mail
• Advance notification of forthcoming ICV events
• Notification of forthcoming national and international events
• Access to the Central School of Speech and Drama with reference only rights (CSSD students have full loan rights), inclusive of access to ICV archive materials.

A copy of an up-to-date CV and Student ID must accompany all applications for Student membership.

[*All applications for membership to the International Centre for Voice are at the discretion of the International Centre for Voice Advisory Board]

Yearly Membership Subscription

Full Individual – £50.00 (£55.00 overseas)
Full Institution – £100.00 (£105.00 overseas)
Student – £20.00 (£25.00 overseas)
Associate – £20.00 (£25.00 overseas)

If you would like to register your interest in The International Centre for Voice and receive further information, please contact: The International Centre for Voice, Central School of Speech and Drama, Embassy Theatre, Eton Avenue, London, NW3 3HY, UK. Telephone: +44 (0)20 7559 3914, fax: +44 (0)20 7722 8183, e-mail: voice@cssd.ac.uk

Appendix 6 – Abbreviations used

ACM – Academy of Contemporary Music
ALRA – Academy of Live and Recorded Arts
BVA –British Voice Association
CSSD – Central School of Speech and Drama
FE –Further Education
HE – Higher Education
ICV – International Centre for Voice
ITT – Initial Teacher Training
LAMDA – London Academy of Music and Dramatic Arts
MAVS – MA in Voice Studies (at CSSD)
NQT – Newly Qualified Teachers
RADA – Royal Academy of Dramatic Arts
RP – Received Pronounciation
RSAMD – Royal Scottish Academy of Music and Drama
RWCMD – Royal Welsh College of Music and Drama
VASTA - Voice and Speech Trainers' Association
VCN – Voice Care Network

(Footnotes)
1 A bellows-operated 'Acoustic-Mechanical Speech Machine' by Wolfgang von Kempelen of Vienna, Austria, described in his 1791 paper Mechanismus der menschlichen Sprache nebst der Beschreibung seiner sprechenden Maschine ("mechanism of the human speech with description of its speaking machine", J.B. Degen, Wien). This machine added models of the tongue and lips, enabling it to produce consonants as well as vowels. [http://en.wikipedia.org/wiki/Speech_synthesis]